T0020911

A JOURNALING DEVOTIONAL

A
FRUITFUL
LIFE

A 45-DAY JOURNEY
through the FRUIT of the SPIRIT

YAHAIRA RAMOS

B&H
PUBLISHING
NASHVILLE, TENNESSEE

Copyright © 2022 by Yahaira Ramos
All rights reserved.
Printed in the United States of America

978-1-0877-4708-8

Published by B&H Publishing Group
Nashville, Tennessee

Dewey Decimal Classification: 234.12
Subject Heading: DEVOTIONAL LITERATURE /
SPIRITUAL GIFTS / CHRISTIAN LIFE

Unless otherwise noted, all Scripture references are taken from the Christian Standard Bible. Copyright © 2017 by Holman Bible Publishers. Used by permission. Christian Standard Bible®, and CSB® are federally registered trademarks of Holman Bible Publishers, all rights reserved.

Scripture references marked ESV are taken from the ESV® Text Edition: 2016. Copyright © 2001 by Crossway Bibles, a publishing ministry of Good News Publishers.

Scripture references marked NIV are taken from the New International Version®, NIV® Copyright ©1973, 1978, 1984, 2011 by Biblica, Inc.® Used by permission. All rights reserved worldwide.

Scripture references marked NLT are taken from the New Living Translation, copyright © 1996, 2004, 2015 by Tyndale House Foundation. Used by permission of Tyndale House Publishers, Inc., Carol Stream, Illinois 60188. All rights reserved.

Scripture references marked NASB1995 are taken from the New American Standard Bible®, Copyright © 1960, 1971, 1977, 1995 by The Lockman Foundation. All rights reserved.

Scripture references marked CEV are taken from the Contemporary English Version, copyright © 1995 by American Bible Society For more information about CEV, visit www.bibles.com and www.cev.bible.

Scripture references marked MSG are taken from The Message, copyright © 1993, 2002, 2018 by Eugene H. Peterson.

Scripture references marked AMP are taken from the Amplified Bible, copyright © 2015 by The Lockman Foundation, La Habra, CA 90631. All rights reserved.

Cover design by Jennifer Allison, Studio Nth.
Cover Images by Ozornina Kseniia/shutterstock and TWINS DESIGN STUDIO/shutterstock. Author photo by Stephy Perea.

1 2 3 4 5 6 • 26 25 24 23 22

To the Lord, to my husband, to my children

CONTENTS

INTRODUCTION

But the fruit of the Spirit is **love**, **joy**, **peace**, **patience**, **kindness**, **goodness**, **faithfulness**, **gentleness**, and **self-control**. The law is not against such things.

GALATIANS 5:22–23, EMPHASIS ADDED

Fruitfulness—how would you define it?

> A big family?
>
> An overflowing bank account?
>
> A job that offers endless possibilities for advancement?
>
> An abundant ministry?

While there are certainly aspects of life that can be fruitful on the outside, the Bible elevates God's most fruitful work in our lives as something that He does on the inside. Through His Spirit, God makes us fruitful from the inside out, cultivating the famous fruit found in Galatians 5: love, joy, peace, patience, kindness, goodness, faithfulness, gentleness, and self-control.

In this beautiful 45-day journaling devotional, we will journey together to explore each fruit of the Spirit that God is bearing in you, right here and right now. No matter what life might look like for you in this season, take heart in knowing that God is doing a work in and through you—a fruitful work.

So what should we know about the fruit of the Spirit before embarking on this journey? Here are some things to keep in mind:

What the Fruit of the Spirit Actually Is. While we all know the specifics of each fruit of the Spirit (Gal. 5 gives us a clear list!), what is the fruit of the Spirit in *general*? Are love, joy, peace, and the rest of the list all just positive things we should try to implement in our lives? Are they randomly picked from a word bank of nice-sounding phrases? No, the fruit of the Spirit is actually the characteristics of God made manifest in His people—in you and me! The Spirit of God takes what's true of God on a character-level, and bears out those things in us, so that our character starts looking more and more like His.

> God is love, so His Spirit makes us more loving, like Him.
>
> Our God is joyful, so His Spirit makes us more joyful, like Him.
>
> Our God is peaceful, patient, kind, good, gentle, and controlled—and, you guessed it, His Spirit's job is to bear all those qualities out in our hearts and minds, so that we might be more like Him!

Who the Fruit-Bearer Is. There's a reason the Bible calls this the fruit of the *Spirit*. The Holy Spirit indwells us when we come to faith in Christ, and He brings along qualities of God with Him because He *is* God. Once God the Holy Spirit indwells us, He then begins His work of producing godly qualities in us. Only *He* is the fruit-bearer! We can cooperate with Him as He cultivates these things in us, of course. But God's Spirit bears the fruit!

The Holy Spirit's Job. While we're on the topic of the Holy Spirit, it would serve us well to stop and ask what the Holy Spirit's job is. There are many answers to that question, but for the purposes of this devotional, it's helpful to point out that one of the tasks of the Holy Spirit is to make us more like Jesus over time. So as we grow in our faith, we should see more of these "fruitful" qualities in our character. Be encouraged, friend: as we develop over time in the Christian life, we aren't simply becoming "nicer," we are becoming more like *Jesus*! What's more, as the Spirit changes us to reflect Jesus's character, He does so on the deep, internal, core level. What I mean is this: we all can do nice deeds from time to time, sure. But plenty of people can do a decent deed with the wrong heart. They can do it for applause. They can do it for convenience. They can do it to pay off some sense of guilt. But not the Christian! The Spirit's job is to change you on a level deeper than just your outer performance. The Holy Spirit bears *internal* fruits of the heart—things we can't fake. He can not only help you do a decent deed, He can transform you to the point that you're doing it for the right reasons. The world can do nice things with their hands, but the Spirit can make a person truly kind *at heart*. Amazing!

What the Fruit of the Spirit Isn't. As we explore each fruit of the Spirit, it might be tempting to start viewing them as an external set of rules or to-dos. But that's not what they are about! They are a transformative, internal work that God does in us from the inside out. Yes, they *affect* what we do on the outside, and we have to work at cooperating with the Spirit as He cultivates them in us, but they aren't rules. They are ways God's character is being developed inside of us!

Our Part to Play. As I've mentioned before, yes, it's the Spirit's job to work out each fruit in us. We could never do it ourselves! But that doesn't mean we don't cooperate with the Spirit and work in tandem with Him. We all have a part to play when it comes to our Christian growth. We can either buck against the work we sense the Spirit doing in us, or we can yield to it, and watch Him guide and transform us! Sometimes operating in love, joy, peace, patience, and all the other fruit is *hard*. And we have some things working against us: the sway of our surrounding society, the enemy, and our own flesh! But the Spirit is stronger than all of those things. If we were born again in conversion through His power to regenerate our hearts, then we are surely able to walk in step with Him all the days after that! Our job is simply to trust Him in faith and believe He can change us.

So, friend, are you ready? Let's get to it!

Much love,
Yahaira Ramos, author and founder of Fruitful Girl

HOW TO USE THIS DEVOTIONAL AND WHAT TO EXPECT

Before we start our journey together through the fruit of the Spirit, let's take a moment to orient ourselves to what is ahead. As we explore each fruit of the Spirit in this devotional, here's what you can expect. Since there are nine particular fruits of the Spirit mentioned in our guiding verses, Galatians 5:22–23, we will go through them in a **nine-week format**.

In any given week, **Days 1–5** will offer you devotional reflections on that week's particular fruit, where we will examine it from various angles, consider various passages of Scripture, and enjoy warm encouragement together from the Lord. **Days 6–7** are reflection days, giving you some breathing space, where you can process, meditate, and journal through what you've learned so far with some promptings, questions, and room for free-style reflection.

In each week, as a new fruit is presented to you, you'll notice something right away—it starts with *God* before it moves on to *us*. That's on purpose! Many times, we forget that the reason God is able to produce love, joy, peace, patience, kindness, goodness, faithfulness, gentleness, and self-control in us is because these things are true of *Him* first. *He bears in us what is true of Himself, so that we look more like Him!*

After we consider how God possesses each fruit Himself (**Day 1**), we will then move on to consider the various ways that fruit should be bearing out in our own lives (**Days 2–5**).

All right! Now that you have a heading for the road ahead, let's not waste another moment. Let's start the journey together, and watch God do a fruitful work in us that only He can do!

GOD'S LOVE FOR US

LOVE // DAY 1

But God demonstrates his own love for us in this:
While we were still sinners, Christ died for us.

ROMANS 5:8 (NIV)

We all know that love is so important in this life. But did you know that love is also one of the most vital subjects in the Bible? We know this because love is mentioned more than 500 times in Scripture! It's not a coincidence that in the famous "fruit of the Spirit" passage, Galatians 5:22–23, love is the first thing listed. Why, you might wonder? Because all the fruit a Christian bears in this life flows from love. It is the greatest of them all, and it makes all of them possible.

God has shown up in my life—and in your life too, I'm sure. Do you remember how you came to Him? I sure do. I was around nine years old when a family member I had never met searched for my family. She was a distant relative, and my parents had no contact. I don't believe she knew that my mother was having a hard time in her marriage, and my father's addictions were taking all the faith she could muster. I don't think she knew that a nine-year-old had seen it all—things she never should have seen as a child—and was also hurting from everything she had experienced in her own family.

But God knew. God knew what I had seen and what my family was going through. So He did what Romans 5:8 tells us about God: He didn't merely *feel* love for my family, He *demonstrated* that love by sending someone to us to help in a time of need.

When I met this family member, she was different. She was loving and had a way of talking to you, with so much intention, love, patience, and kindness. At first, in my confused nine-year-old mind, I thought she was being fake, and I judged her. I had never experienced something like that from a total stranger, and I didn't know how to interpret such light, given how much darkness I was walking through. Like walking out of a movie theater in broad daylight after being in the dark for hours, I winced and recoiled from the light in her at first. But eventually I saw she was reflecting God's love. And I wanted what she had. I wanted God's love that radiated in her life to radiate in my own life from then on.

My first experience of love from a total stranger was the love that I needed. God's love was near, and I liked it. Over time, this family member took the time to share the gospel with my mother, and the impact she made in my life hit an all-time high. God's love spoke to me loud and clear. At my young age, I learned that Christ died for me and all the sin in the world. And I didn't just learn this as if it were facts listed in a textbook. I knew it was more personal than that. I could feel, deep down, in a personal way that apart from God, I wasn't a good kid. Somehow I knew I had sin that needed dealing with—this was a pain I could feel in my bones. And this family member helped me learn that Christ could be the one to deal with it.

After the gospel was shared with her, I got to witness my mom give her life to Christ, right in front of me. And her decision impacted me for a lifetime. I did the same two weeks later. I received Jesus as my Lord and Savior. And all that pain over my sin that I had been carrying—it was gone.

For the first time, I didn't just know about the love God had for the world. I *felt* the love He had for *me*, and God took away the burdens I carried. He hadn't just sent a family member to show me He loved me; He had also sent someone greater—His only *Son*—to show me His love.

That's what God does. He *demonstrates* His love. And that love searched me, found me, and made me new. It did not change my problems at home, but it prepared me for what I would face in my future. At nine years old, I learned that He had died for me before my existence. I knew that His love lived in me, and I finally understood the root of real love.

The true source of love is God, demonstrated in His Son's death. Christ came for us out of love, and the Father's love was the seed. His plan to give us righteousness and salvation through Christ was motivated by love. Without His plan of love to rescue us, we wouldn't have salvation. Only God Himself could pay the price to save us.

Isn't that good news today? Love starts with God because He loved us first. He loved you before you loved Him. He has given Himself to you. And that makes all the difference when it comes to bearing the fruit of love in our own lives. We can't bear any fruit of love toward others until we understand just how much He loves us. Will you trust in that love today?

PRAYER: Lord, You are the dealer and the definition of love. Your love is active, pure, kind, intentional, marvelous, and demonstrated for us clearly on the cross. There is no one like You, and we are thankful for the love You give us because it is comforting and it casts out our fear. Jesus, thank You for pouring out Your own life for us while we were still sinners, hurting in our darkest moments. Thank You for making a way to seek and find us when we had no hope. Father, like You sent Your Son, send us into the lives of others, and let us be a vessel that connects people to Your great love and Your gospel. In Jesus's name, Amen.

REFLECTION QUESTIONS

What does love mean to you?

Who or what do you love most in life? Why?

How does today's verse
change the way you
view love?

_____
_____
_____

_____
_____
_____
_____
_____
_____
_____
_____
_____
_____
_____
_____
_____
_____
_____
_____
_____
_____
_____
_____
_____
_____

**Put in your own
words how God
has demonstrated
His love for you.**

LOVING GOD

LOVE // DAY 2

We love because he first loved us.

1 JOHN 4:19 (NIV)

What's the greatest commandment in the whole Bible? If you've ever read through the Gospels, you know Jesus's answer: to love God not just a little, but with *all we've got* (Matt. 22:37).

Okay. We're supposed to love God with every fiber of our being. But do you ever wonder *how*? Especially on days when we don't feel warm and fuzzy toward God? *How* are we supposed to muster up this love for the Lord?

Through the years, I have had to learn and re-learn *and* re-learn again that, as 1 John 4:19 tells us, God loved me first! As we learned yesterday, God demonstrated His love by sending His own Son to die in my place and give me new life. He did all of that on my behalf *before I was even born*. He. Loved. Me. First! And you know what? He loves you first too.

Isn't this a hard concept to understand as the years go by? When I came to Christ as a little girl, I believed in God's unconditional love. God loved me, and that was that! But something happened as I got older and entered my teens and my twenties—it got harder to believe. Time after time, I would fall short of His grace when things got hard, and I'd feel far away from Him. I'd doubt that His love could meet me in *this* place. But over and over, He would remind me that He knows me better than anybody, that He knew my mistakes, and that His love could reach *even here*.

Do you ever find yourself amazed by this? God just keeps on loving us. He keeps showing up to help us along. Oftentimes, I ask myself why? And how is this possible? I am not worthy of His love—none of us are. But then I remember the gospel: through Christ, God sees us differently than we see ourselves. He sees things we can't see. Instead of seeing us as totally compromised by sin, He now sees us as "wonderfully made" (Ps. 139:14 NIV). Instead of seeing us as enemies, He sees us as children. Instead of seeing us as deserving of His judgment, He sees us as receptacles of His love. He gazes on us with the same favor He bestows on His own Son! Ultimately, because of Jesus's work on the cross and declaration that "it is finished," the way God sees us is a complete us, not broken, but made right in Christ.

The idea of God loving us first is just the beginning of His mercy and grace toward us. He didn't just love us before we loved Him. He *knew* us before we knew Him. He knows everything about us and still loves us. He knows the darkest places in our lives, hearts, and minds, and yet He still loves us—it is mind-blowing!

So how do we love God with all we've got? We accept that we are sinful and need His love, and then we receive His gift of life. And then, on the days we forget we've received such an extravagant love, we let Him remind us of it. By doing these things, we love Him back—it is just that simple.

And where can we find these reminders? Where can we find out who He is, being reminded that He is the beginning and the end, that He gives and takes away for our good according to His will, that He is the one that gives life, and that His love never ends for us? Where can we go to remember He is our creator, and we are His creation, that He has called us His children, He knows us by name and knows what we need before we know our own need? Where can we run to be reminded He has a plan for us that is different than the one we have? One way is through His Word—the Bible! Friend, when you need a fresh reminder of how He loves you, run to what He's revealed to you in His Word. There you will find His love on full display! And as you take this in, you'll experience His fountain of love overflowing from your heart outward toward Him and toward others. You may have come in as an empty and broken cup, but by meditation on His love for you as seen in the Scriptures, He can restore and fill you up! We are bare without Him. But with Him, we overflow in love.

There's another way we can be reminded of God's love for us—through His Spirit who lives in us! Even though you are flawed, the Spirit can remind you God loves you unconditionally. He can give you the desire to please Him. He can keep you aligned and close with God. He can convict you and help you remember that to love Jesus is not just to feel something warm and encouraging on an emotional level, but to obey His instruction on a practical level (John 14:15). In other words, the act of obedience is God's love language—and the Spirit can help you speak that language! *He is the one who bears the fruit of love in your life!*

We love God because He loved us first. He loved us first by sending His Son, by giving us His Word, and by giving us His Spirit. Friend, *He has given you more than enough resources to love Him with all you've got!* Walk in those resources today!

PRAYER: Heavenly Father, You are all-knowing and all-loving. Thank You for loving me first! You have gone to great lengths to show the love You have for me. Help me check my striving at the door and understand I can't love You on my own—I need You and Your love to fill my heart to the point of overflow. Thank You for giving me Your Son, Your Word, and Your Spirit to help me love You with all I've got! Help me continue to return to these resources in the moments I forget Your love. Thank You, Lord. In Jesus's name, Amen.

REFLECTION QUESTIONS

Before today, did you think loving God was something you had to muster up all on your own? What was it like?

What is your definition of obedience to God?

How is love connected to obedience?

_____

_____

_____

_____

_____

_____

_____

_____

_____

_____

_____

_____

_____

_____

_____

_____

_____

_____

_____

_____

_____

_____

_____

_____

_____

_____

_____

In what specific ways might God be asking you to show your love for Him?

_____

_____

_____

LOVING OTHERS

LOVE // DAY 3

[The lawyer] answered, "Love the Lord your God with all your heart and with all your soul and with all your strength and with all your mind"; and, "Love your neighbor as yourself." "You have answered correctly," Jesus replied. "Do this and you will live." But he wanted to justify himself, so he asked Jesus, "And who is my neighbor?"

In reply Jesus said: "A man was going down from Jerusalem to Jericho, when he was attacked by robbers. They stripped him of his clothes, beat him and went away, leaving him half dead. A priest happened to be going down the same road, and when he saw the man, he passed by on the other side. So too, a Levite, when he came to the place and saw him, passed by on the other side. But a Samaritan, as he traveled, came where the man was; and when he saw him, he took pity on him. He went to him and bandaged his wounds, pouring on oil and wine. Then he put the man on his own donkey, brought him to an inn and took care of him. The next day he took out two denarii and gave them to the innkeeper. 'Look after him,' he said, 'and when I return, I will reimburse you for any extra expense you may have.' Which of these three do you think was a neighbor to the man who fell into the hands of robbers?"

The expert in the law replied, "The one who had mercy on him." Jesus told him, "Go and do likewise."

LUKE 10:27–37 (NIV)

Yesterday we learned that love for God is something that can fill us to the point of overflow—His love pouring through us onto others. And when we think of "loving others" in a generic sense, we nod along, don't we? I highly doubt there are any Christians in the world who think loving other people is a bad thing.

But here's where Scripture steps on our toes. While we all agree loving other people is good, there's an inquisitive young expert in the Law who comes asking a most telling question in Luke 10: *Sure, we should love our neighbor, but who exactly is our neighbor, and what exactly does loving them mean?*

Re-read the verses above. Do you see what Jesus's parable of the Good Samaritan reveals to us? Your neighbor is *anyone* who comes across your path in need! Friend or stranger, respected in society or despised, it doesn't matter.

Following Jesus's teaching here means to love everyone. You are reading this right: EVERYONE! You might wonder how this task could be asked of you, but remember, the Holy Spirit enables us to love more than what we think is possible. We might not be asked to die for others in a literal way, but Jesus's example teaches us to die to our flesh so that we might love others well. And what did that look like for the Good Samaritan? Did it look like just *feeling* love for the beat-down man on the side of the road? Or did it look like something else?

If you look closely, you'll see the Good Samaritan's love wasn't just *felt* with the heart; it was *demonstrated* with actions. Instead of passing by, he stops. Instead of leaving the man bleeding, he bandages his wounds. More than that, he cares for the wounds with oil and wine—expensive! The Samaritan could have just left the wounded man there to heal, but he goes even further, giving the man his own animal to ride on and paying for him to recover in a costly hotel (two denarii is two days' worth of wages!). In Jesus's mind, loving others doesn't look like mere feelings; it looks like active and costly *sacrifice*.

I still struggle with loving everyone in this way, but here are ways I test my own fruitfulness in the Spirit when a "neighbor" in need crosses my path: first, I am now quick to rebuke and correct myself when I want to pass by instead of stop and help. Second, I try to see them with spiritual eyes—the way God sees them, so I might grow in His compassion. Then, I give them some sort of resource I have, just as many others have done for me in my life. Maybe it's my time, my encouragement, a meal, some money, or a compliment with love. Finally, I pray for them and me.

I heard someone say once, "If you don't like someone, remember you have more in common than you think." And think about it—even if I don't believe I could have anything in common with certain neighbors in my life, I know we always have one thing in common: Jesus died for our sins!

Perhaps loving everyone is hard for you. I imagine that maybe rejection is the thing holding you back from loving someone. I get that. We face a lot of rejection in our society these days, don't we? As a little child who journeyed to America as an immigrant, I know all about rejection, but I didn't let that stop me from loving others. To encourage you, let me help you look to this truth: Christ reminds us He, too, was rejected. He had to be rejected first and greatly to save us (Mark 9:12). He was rejected by His own people—they would not receive Him (John 1:11). And yet He died for them and for us, giving us the hope today we possess!

Remember this, friend: *it took Jesus dying for me and changing me from the inside out to transform me into a person who is capable of truly loving other people.* I believe that simple reminder helps me correct my heart and dig deep, not for the love *I* have for my neighbor, but for that love *God* has for them. When I remind myself that "Christ died for *us*"—meaning not just me, but them *and* me—I finally experience the power to love my neighbor in a costly way. Only His love can produce this kind of sacrifice!

PRAYER: Abba, Father, thank You for the hope I possess because of Your Son's sacrifice for me. When I was left for dead on the side of the road, He crossed over and saved me! What a costly act! You are the enabler of all love—help me extend Your love in this sacrificial way to anyone and everyone, even those I'd usually ignore. Help me remember that no matter the neighbor who crosses my path, Christ died for us both! Let the Spirit enrich me with this love and empower me to cross to the other side of the road so that I might serve others in Your name. Help me love like You and grow in Your ways. In Jesus's name, Amen.

REFLECTION QUESTIONS

What obstacle is in the way of extending costly love toward those you consider inconvenient, annoying, or unworthy? Rejection? Fear? Apathy? Hatred?

What can you do differently this week to take a "next step" toward sacrificial love?

What resources are you most protective of, or most unwilling to offer your neighbor? Why? How does Jesus's teaching challenge this?

_____

_____

_____

_____

_____

_____

_____

_____

_____

_____

_____

_____

_____

_____

_____

_____

_____

_____

_____

_____

_____

_____

_____

_____

_____

_____

_____

What did God reveal to you today in the story of the Good Samaritan?

_____

_____

_____

LOVING OUR ENEMIES

LOVE // DAY 4

"But I say to you who listen: Love your enemies, do what is good to those who hate you, bless those who curse you, pray for those who mistreat you. If anyone hits you on the cheek, offer the other also. And if anyone takes away your coat, don't hold back your shirt either. Give to everyone who asks you, and from someone who takes your things, don't ask for them back. Just as you want others to do for you, do the same for them. If you love those who love you, what credit is that to you? Even sinners love those who love them. If you do what is good to those who are good to you, what credit is that to you? Even sinners do that. And if you lend to those from whom you expect to receive, what credit is that to you? Even sinners lend to sinners to be repaid in full. *But love your enemies, do what is good, and lend, expecting nothing in return. Then your reward will be great, and you will be children of the Most High.* For he is gracious to the ungrateful and evil. Be merciful, just as your Father also is merciful."

LUKE 6:27–36 (EMPHASIS ADDED)

When you think of the "others" in your life whom you love dearly, what faces come to mind? Your kids? Your friends? Your spouse? Your roommates? The people who love you back?

That seems natural enough. Those are the faces that come to my mind, too. But according to Jesus, *anyone* can love those they hold dear, and *anyone* can love those who love them back. But a Christian who is bearing the fruit of the Spirit isn't just anyone! For the believer who is empowered by the Spirit of God, loving others goes beyond what's natural into the supernatural. It goes from loving those we already like, to loving those we don't like, to those we outright hate.

But how do we get there? How do we love others in a "beyond natural" way? Great question. We must run to the Scriptures for Jesus's example and His power. He loved all sorts of people, but most unexpectedly, He loved the people who wanted to kill Him, even asking that God might forgive them in the moments they jeered at Him and nailed Him to a cross! What's more incredible—*we* are part of that crowd. That's right. Scripture says *you and I* were God's enemies before He saved us in Christ (Rom. 5:10). And yet He still came for us. This means that Jesus loved not just the enemies in His lifetime, but in all lifetimes—in *our* lifetime. He loved us repeatedly, demonstrating His love toward us even when we once stood against Him. That is the example we want to follow—someone who sacrifices Himself not just for His friends, but for His enemies! His example is everything for us, as is His Spirit who helps us love in this most unnatural way.

If we take another look at the verses above, especially the italicized verses, we notice it is both a commandment to love and a promise, too.

Hopefully, as children of God, we don't have a long list of enemies. But we probably do know difficult people to whom we can extend our love and mercy just as Jesus did to us, even at our worst! Truthfully it can be challenging for us to love or serve them, but we give it because God's grace has covered us with the same grace and love first. We must remember that God moved toward us when we were evil and ungrateful, extending the hope of the gospel to us. We must go and do likewise, proving we have been changed by His love!

Who is your enemy? Someone who betrayed you? Slandered you? Let you down? Or perhaps it isn't a "someone," but rather a group of people you think are terrible, immoral, ruining our culture, or unworthy of your kindness. Now that you have them in your mind, here's something that might help: ask the Lord to give you the strength to love them as He loves you in your worst moments. I know it may feel like the times have changed so much since this verse was written—perhaps you think the types of people in today's time are truly far worse than the people in Jesus's age. But look into the background of Luke's Gospel, and you'll discover Jesus said these words during times not much different than ours. He and His disciples lived in a moment when ethnic, religious, economic, and social groups divided them. Sound familiar? I guess not much has changed! The Bible speaks loud and clear no matter how many years have passed; Christ's words stand firm and in truth. The Bible is not only relevant today and forever—its words have eternal power to instruct you and change you, even when it comes to your enemy.

In the time of this passage, the most known and influential enemy was the Roman Empire, which ruled harshly and without mercy. But Rome's power was limited—God knew that. Their days in power were numbered. Something the disciples did not understand was that while Rome was not only made up of citizens considered as enemies; it was also made up of citizens who needed to hear the gospel and be saved! God cared for them also. Are you someone's enemy? Are you difficult to love sometimes? Have you hurt anyone at some point? At the bottom of things, what makes us any different from our enemies? We all have compromised hearts before a holy God, unless He interrupts our story with His grace. And transformative gospel power.

The differences that pull us apart can be many, but no differences can separate us from the love of God. Jesus is clear: we are to love our enemy and anyone who crosses our lives: the good, the evil, the rich, the poor, the grateful, and the ungrateful.

Our Lord is powerful; He has no limits and He reigns forever. And so it makes sense that His disciples expected Him to free them from Rome (and conquer Rome), reign over them as king, and rebuild the temple at the drop of a hat. But that was not Jesus's way of doing things. His mission was greater and higher and wider than just what was happening in Rome. He will reign over us all one day, make no mistake about that—but He wanted to save us first. We were once the enemies of heaven, and we walked this earth dead—and the only One who could give us life had to die first. That is *real* love and mercy. He did this for you and me—*us*, His enemies!

And you know what? God has the same heart for enemies. He wants to do the same for them. How will they know of His enemy-loving nature apart from witness? How can they experience this kind of countercultural love if His children refuse to put it on display? Friend, what if He wanted to stretch out His love and compassion and salvation on those who are still His enemies *through you*?

Will you let Him? If knowing all this doesn't make you want to change and treat others as the King of kings has treated you, ask yourself: What will?

Let us remember that when we show love and mercy to others, especially enemies, we show we are different because we are sons and daughters of the Most High. We reveal who our Father is, as we walk and talk and act like Him in this world. Let us remember on top of everything, when we love like God does, we will also enjoy a great reward one day. And let us also remember we aren't so very different from those we are tempted to hate. If there's hope for us, there's hope for them. Let's share it! As we do, we allow the Spirit to bear the fruit of enemy-seeking love!

PRAYER: Thank You, Lord, for loving me—me, who used to be Your enemy! Thank You for Your salvation, Your love, and the mercy You have given me at great price. Thank You for Your fruit-bearing Spirit as well as the examples and instruction You give me in the Scriptures, which teach me how to love those I'm tempted to hate. Only Your grace and Your Spirit make me want to change and be known as Your child. Help me, oh Lord, to stretch out and extend love to others like You do. Overcome any hatred in my heart with love, and help me pour that love out onto my enemies, no matter who they are. Bear this impossible sort of fruit in my heart, even now. In the precious name of Jesus, Amen.

REFLECTION QUESTIONS

In this season of life, what person or group of people would you consider the enemy?

In what ways, deep down, are you and the enemy alike?

What fears do you have about obeying Jesus's command to love your enemy? What truth do you need to believe in order to silence that fear?

_____
_____
_____
_____
_____
_____
_____
_____
_____
_____
_____
_____
_____
_____
_____
_____
_____
_____
_____
_____
_____

What could active mercy look like in your life? What small step can you take to love your enemy today?

_____
_____
_____
_____

LOVING THE LOST
AND THE BROKEN

LOVE // DAY 5

I will seek the lost, bring back the strays, bandage the injured, and strengthen the weak, but I will destroy the fat and the strong. I will shepherd them with justice.

EZEKIEL 34:16

Have you ever gotten lost? Maybe while driving to a vacation in some other state, or on the way to someone's house? Maybe in a mall or at a concert, when you were a child, all alone and afraid, wondering where your parents were?

Being lost is so disorienting. It can even feel like despair. *Which way is the right way? Will I ever find my way home?*

The good news about the love of God is that it stretches to the lost and the broken. It runs toward those who feel like they don't know the way home, or which way is the right way in this world.

Who are the lost? The ones who do not yet know Christ.

Who are the strays? Those who find themselves wandering without a direction or a purpose in life, or those wandering down the path of sin.

Who are the broken? Biblically, they are the hopeless, the physically or mentally ill, or the marginalized. They are those who need someone to reach out and meet their needs.

The Bible tells us that Jesus loves to rescue the lost, heal the broken, and strengthen weak believers so that they might grow. And because of the Spirit, His love is now in us, which means He wants us to love others in these ways too! He wants us to share our faith with the lost and the broken, not keep it to ourselves and turn "strong and fat" (a biblical term for those who keep the nourishment for themselves without sharing it with those who desperately need it). You and I used to be the lost, the broken, and the straying. Yet Jesus helped us find our way home. So let's not hoard Him. Let's share Christ, our Bread of Life, with those who are in need!

Moving beyond a time *you* were lost, now think of a time you encountered someone else who was lost. Have you ever helped someone who asked you for directions to find a classroom, a building, a street, or a freeway? I call these moments a "lifeguard opportunity." What are the chances we get to give them directions? What are the chances God gave *us* the opportunity to speak to them?

I don't believe in chance, do you? The Bible teaches that every encounter is from the Lord. And so, when we come across someone who is spiritually lost, even if for a brief moment, we must remember that the opportunity God is giving us to direct them to Jesus is once-in-a-lifetime. Don't waste it! We have the map in our hands, and they need what we have, Christ, who is "the way, the truth, and the life!" (John 14:6).

I know it is a scary thing to share the gospel with a total stranger, but what are the chances they will see you again? What if it is the only opportunity you or they will have? What if you are the obstacle between God and them? What if you're the only "Jesus" they've ever encountered, or will ever encounter again? What if the Spirit's love flowing through *you* is the way God wants to help them find their path?

The same goes for those who aren't strangers, but are lost and broken friends and family who we know well. What if a longstanding relationship with you is the way God wants to reveal His love for them?

I still remember the first time I shared the gospel: I was so afraid, but I knew I had to stand for Jesus publicly. It didn't go as expected, but I did it—and I survived, and I can't explain the fire inside me to want to do it again. As if the Holy Spirit gave me the energy to repeat it. So I did! I am not going to lie; I was told "no" many times. But each time I remember they didn't reject me; they rejected Christ (Luke 10:16; John 15:18).

What is your story? We all have a unique story, but one thing is similar: Jesus reached for us. He didn't give up on us. He conquered death because we couldn't. He kept reaching, in all sorts of ways, until we came to know these truths for ourselves—until we responded to Him in faith. And now you and I are walking testimonies of what God has done for us. We are the living proof walking. That's our story!

What is the story of the lost and the broken in your life? *It could be the same.* Friend, please do not lose heart for the lost and the broken, for you might be the way Jesus reaches to them. Keep them in your prayers, and when you get the opportunity to share the gospel, let the Holy Spirit guide you, and just do it. Share the Bread of Life with the hungry!

PRAYER: Oh Lord Savior, thank You for what You have done for me. I was once lost without You and found myself hurt by life, and You made a way for me to find the path of life, to be seen and healed by You, to experience new life in Your name. Set me ablaze to share You with those who are lost, straying, and broken like I was. Keep feeding Your fire of love for them through the Holy Spirit in me, and help me to listen when I need to act quickly and share Your gospel to others in need. Give me the heart of Christ—to seek the lost, and point them toward You! Bless my brothers and sisters who are currently obeying You in this, reaching out in love to those You came to save. Multiply my love for the wandering and the wounded through Your Spirit, and help me minister to them in Your name, Amen.

REFLECTION QUESTIONS

Who are the lost, broken, and straying in your life? (Think through your family, friends, community, neighborhood, city, and so on.)

_____

_____

_____

_____

_____

_____

_____

Which of those listed earlier are you most likely to minister to? Which of them do you tend to distance yourself from? Why?

_____

_____

_____

**What is holding you back
from sharing the gospel
with someone today?**

**What does the
"strong and fat" image
mean, according to this verse?
What is one practical step you can
take away from that image?**

REFLECTION AND REST

Use the last two days of this week to rest from reading, and instead, reflect on what you've learned. Use the journaling prompts and space below to process and enjoy what the Lord is doing in your heart.

1. What aspect of God's love did you find most encouraging this week? Most surprising?

_____

_____

_____

_____

_____

_____

_____

_____

2. In what tangible ways do you see the fruit of love being developed by God's Spirit in your heart and actions? Take some time to thank God for this fruitful work He's doing in you.

_____

_____

_____

_____

_____

_____

_____

_____

_____

3. In this season of your life, which of these needs the most development in your heart? Circle one.

Loving God.   Loving Others.   Loving Enemies.   Loving the Lost and Broken.

What are some practical next steps you can take to develop this?

_____

_____

_____

_____

_____

_____

_____

_____

_____

_____

FREESTYLE REFLECTION

Use this space below to pray, write out a meaningful passage of Scripture, or process anything God has placed on your heart this week.

GOD'S JOY

JOY // DAY 1

And a voice from heaven said,
"This is my dearly loved Son, who brings me great joy."

MATTHEW 3:17 (NLT)

I don't know about you, but when I think of joy, I think of it mostly as something *we're* supposed to have as Christians. I don't always think of it as something *God* possesses. But Scripture reveals that He does!

What does our Father delight in? What brings Him joy?

There are many answers to that question, but the important answer is this: His Son!

I can almost picture the sky opening as the Lord speaks here in the moment of Jesus's baptism. I can imagine the clouds spreading out as the sun breaks in, beaming brightly through them, over the water. I can almost hear that fatherly voice calling down, declaring pure joy over His one and only Son. I can picture Jesus coming up from the water, shining and glistening in the sun, and probably smiling from hearing His Father's voice of pleasure.

What absolute joy it is to listen to your Father's happy voice loud and clear.

Can you remember a time when someone pointed you out of the crowd or sang your praises publicly, declaring how loved and important you are to them? It fills you with joy.

Some of us can remember this sort of moment. Others of us have to *imagine* it, because we can't recall a moment when someone delighted in us to the point of singing or shouting. Especially not from a dad.

I speak from experience. My father had a drug problem for most of my life, and I did not have the relationship I wish I had had with him. He just wasn't a present father. I would have given anything for him to come to my track or cross-country competitions as a teen. I wish I could have heard him cheer me, screaming front and center in the crowd.

While that absence in my life is a painful one, there is good news: I came to know Christ by that point, God's highest joy becoming my highest joy too. So the most important thing for me to remember in every competition I ran was that my heavenly Father was there with me. In His fatherly kindness, He found a way to communicate His delight in me, even though the vessel He chose was not my earthly dad.

I remember strangers telling me the great job I did out there, and coaches telling me how proud they were of me. I remember those beautiful 5 a.m. practices when I saw the sunrise and the sky move. I remember when I wanted to give up, and He gave me the strength to keep going. It sounds wild, but I know that in those moments, God was declaring His joy over me. Whether through the sky or the words of others or the strength I needed to run, He found a way to show me He is not an absent God, nor a mean one, but a God of delight who takes joy in His children to the same degree He takes joy in His own Son! In all these ways and more, He spoke to me as nobody could, and every day He gave me Jesus, the portion of His joy. I cannot describe how much it meant to me, and nobody can take those memories, nor His favor, from me.

[Presently, you'll be delighted to know that my earthly father is now clean from his drug use and, even better, is a believer (though I am no longer a runner, ha!). After all our family went through, it is worth everything to know God was not only near me; He was working slowly in the heart of my dad too. What a joy to see my father not just clean, but saved by God's grace—another child to delight in!]

So, friend, know this: the Lord's joy over you might not come through the vessels you want it to, but He is declaring it. If you're in Christ, He radiates the same joy over you that He did in His Son on this beautiful day of baptism.

You may be asking yourself, *But what is it about Jesus that brings God joy?* On one hand, it is because Jesus is His Son, who the Father has delighted in for eternity past. (In the Trinity, we could say God delights in Himself and experiences all the joy in the world without anyone else's help! It's part of His nature; joy just flows out of Him without effort!) But another big reason why God was so pleased with His Son is because Jesus was about to begin His ministry, where He was going to save and pay for the ransom of many. Through His gospel work on the cross and in the resurrection, Jesus was about to go bring many more "sons and daughters to glory" (Heb. 2:10).

Want to know what else brings God joy? His creation. Yes, I am talking about nature (Gen. 1:31). But I'm also talking about more than just plants and rocks. *We* are His creation, and He loves us so much. Zephaniah puts it this way: "The LORD your God is in your midst, a victorious warrior. He will exult over you with joy, He will be quiet in His love *[meaning He won't mention your past sins!]*, He will rejoice over you with shouts of joy" (Zeph. 3:17 NASB1995).

And yet there's even more joy in God's heart. Another thing God rejoices in is the moment lost souls receive the gift of His Son. His heavenly dwelling celebrates in a next-level way when one lost sinner repents, trusting in Jesus for salvation (Luke 15:7, 32). As we walked out of darkness and death, into light and life, the Scriptures say, "he brought his people out with joy, his chosen ones with singing" (Ps. 105:43 ESV). He rejoices with singing every time a new believer comes to faith in Him!

Another thing that brings God pleasure and joy is when we mature as His followers and bear fruit in His name. When you not only believe His teachings, but *abide* in them and obey them, His joy explodes and your joy is made full too (John 15:11)! We can bring so much glory to the Father by bearing fruit, proving we are true disciples of Christ (John 15:8).

God doesn't expect you to muster up joy all on your own. He wants *His* ever-flowing joy to be in you (John 15:11). And as we've seen, that's a lot of joy! As we walk forward today, let's remember together that our God is not a god of misery—but a God of delight who is able to help us not only experience His joy, but bear it out in our lives toward others through His Spirit.

PRAYER: Oh Lord, thank You for being a God of great joy! Thank You for the joy I have been given in Christ Jesus. I pray You'll help me remember that joy is something that originates in You, not something I can produce on my own. When I am tempted to find joy in what I have or don't have, I pray You'll convict me and bring me back to the joy that is found only in You. Help me rejoice in the things You do—in Your world, in Your people, in lost souls finding salvation, and most importantly, in Your Son! In Jesus's name, Amen.

REFLECTION QUESTIONS

When you think of God, do you picture Him as a delightful God—as a heavenly Father bursting with joy? Why or why not?

_____

_____

_____

_____

_____

_____

_____

_____

_____

_____

_____

_____

_____

_____

_____

_____

_____

_____

_____

_____

_____

_____

When you feel low, what do you usually run to so that you might find joy?

Why do you think you don't immediately run to God for joy in those moments? In what ways is He a better place to run?

_____

_____

_____

_____

_____

_____

_____

_____

_____

_____

_____

_____

_____

_____

_____

_____

_____

_____

_____

_____

_____

_____

_____

Have you ever tried to live the "joyful Christian life" in your own strength, only to be exhausted by the effort? What have you learned today that might help with this tendency?

_____

_____

_____

_____

THE JOY SET
BEFORE CHRIST

JOY // DAY 2

Let us also lay aside every encumbrance and the sin which so easily
entangles us, and let us run with endurance the race that is set before
us, fixing our eyes on Jesus, the author and perfecter of faith, who
for the joy set before Him endured the cross, despising the shame,
and has sat down at the right hand of the throne of God.

HEBREWS 12:1–2 (NASB1995)

Have you ever been in some sort of race, and midway through, lost focus?
Maybe it was a literal race where you ran a 5k and got really tired in
certain moments, looking to the left and the right so you could cast your
gaze *anywhere else* but that pavement you'd been staring at for what feels
like forever. Maybe it was a metaphorical race—a race to the top of your
job's corporate ladder, or a race to some weight loss goal you had (if we'd
only stay the course and keep away from the cookie cabinet!).

I have experienced this many times too—even while writing this
book. It is not hard to lose focus, because slowing down or taking a break
or looking around instead of toward the finish line is just . . . easier. The
things that are worth waiting for, well, they take time and effort on our
part.

The Christian walk is no different. It is not easy, but we accept the
challenge of running the race of faith because we know who waits for us at
the finish line. We know that we will face hardship, but that builds us up
to greater spiritual maturity and overall character.

Hardship. Challenge. Effort. These are not words we like to hear! Is
this all the Christian life is? No, friend! We forget something that lies right
in the middle of all that difficulty: joy.

How can we know this? Because we treat our race of faith like Jesus treated His. In Hebrews 12:1–2, we see that although Jesus had to endure the cross and take on its humiliation and shame, He did it for a reason—*joy*! "For the *joy* set before him" (NIV, emphasis added), Christ faced the cross, died in our place, and resurrected. Joy is what motivated Him and met Him in those hard moments of fulfilling His Father's plan.

Joy about what? you might ask. The joy that was "set before him" means this: Jesus endured all the hard stuff because of what awaited Him on the other side. He kept going because He knew two things: one, His work was going to bring us safely to the other side of our sin, where it was finally paid for and we got to be made right with the Father. Two, He knew the glory the Father was going to bestow upon Him on the other side of the resurrection. In short, He kept going because He knew His reward was waiting after all this hard stuff was said and done—the reward of His own exaltation, the reward of His reunification with the Father, and the reward of new brothers and sisters being given the very same things!

Jesus wasn't happy about the agony of the cross, of course. Fleeting happiness is not what got Him through. *The joy of what the agony would accomplish is what got Him through.*

Personally, that hits home for me. As a child, I had to grow up faster than other children my age. (I genuinely feel ten years older than I should—can you relate?) I was the oldest of three siblings in a household where one parent not only had an addiction problem, as I've mentioned before, but also a violent temper. I tried to protect them as much as possible from our circumstances. My mother had her own problems, too, but always found a way to protect us while being a victim of domestic violence. I often had to get in the middle of them to set them apart and try to break it up. I remember the agony, crying so much that my lungs and heart were in excruciating pain. It wasn't just physical; my soul ached too. In those moments, the Lord truly met me and helped me sense that I was not hurting alone; He was hurting for this too.

I asked the Lord for a way out of it, saying, "I did not ask for this, Lord. Please help me." I asked Him to come to save me. Little did I know *He had*, and *He did*. Growing up as an inconsistent Catholic who didn't read (or have) a Bible, I knew nothing of a personal relationship with God. I was lost, and I didn't know where to run or focus instead. I just wanted happiness for my family. I thought that was the problem. I thought happiness was going to fix us. But happiness comes and goes because it is temporary.

God wanted joy for me. He wants joy for you. And once I finally became a Christian, I began to understand passages like Hebrews 12:1–2. I began to understand that you can be in a painful situation, but you endure it for the joy on the other side. For me and my mom, I endured the hard moments for the sake of getting my siblings through it unharmed. I wasn't happy about the violent situation we were in. But because I knew what my agony would accomplish, I stayed the course and helped them through. For the joy set before me—their protection and safety on the other side—I endured.

Or consider the example is the joy moms experience in birthing a child. For me, one of the most refining and rewarding moments of joy in my life was giving birth and finally having a baby in my arms. Labor pain is like breaking every bone in your body, but after that, you are given a gift of pure joy. I found joy when I was holding my child—what was on the other side was worth the pain. New life. I still remember the words I said: "Thank You, Lord. Thank You, Jesus." For my child was a God-given miracle.

God wants to develop that kind of joy in your life. One that endures for the sake of what's on the other side. It's something that nobody but Jesus can give you, and nobody can take away. Keep your eyes on Jesus, friend. He—the one who gave His life, the one who always strives to accomplish the Father's master plan, the one who is the author and perfecter of our faith, the one who knew His mission and didn't lose focus to see it through, the one who endured the humiliation, shame, and death of a cross on our behalf, the one who resurrected, the one who has total authority and now sits at the right hand of God in majesty—*He* is the absolute joy. And His example shows you just how far joy will take you, and just how much it can get you through. Through His Spirit, let Him bear this kind of joy in you so that you might run your race with endurance all the way to the other side!

PRAYER: Oh Jesus, thank You for finding it pure joy to endure the cross on my behalf. Thank You for enduring agony so I might get to the other side of life safely. I pray You produce the same kind of joy in me. Help me find the joy set before me. I ask for patience in the plans ahead of me, as I face many challenges. Help me abide in You so I can overcome. Help me keep my eyes on You, the author, and perfecter of my faith, as I grow in spiritual maturity and character for Your glory. Keep me running toward You, and keep my eyes focused on the mission at hand. Whatever agony I might face, give me the strength I need to face it with joy. I ask this in Your Holy name, Jesus's name, Amen.

REFLECTION QUESTIONS

How does the world define *joy*? How is it different than the way the Bible defines it?

What difficult situation do you face today? How does today's passage speak to this situation with it comes to joy?

How is it possible that Jesus considered going to the cross a "joy"? Explain this in your own words.

_____

_____

_____

_____

_____

_____

_____

_____

_____

_____

_____

_____

_____

_____

_____

_____

_____

_____

_____

_____

_____

_____

_____

_____

What usually distracts you from running the Christian race with total focus? How might today's lesson help you in those future moments of distraction?

JOY IN THE
GOOD SEASONS

JOY // DAY 3

And they kept the Feast of Unleavened Bread seven days with joy, for the LORD had made them joyful and had turned the heart of the king of Assyria to them, so that he aided them in the work of the house of God, the God of Israel.

———————

EZRA 6:22 (ESV)

Are you a fan of long celebrations? Maybe I'm the only one in the world, but I am not a fan of parties that last a long time. Usually it's because with all of the fun, there's a lot of anxiety happening too. Lots of logistics to juggle, people to direct, and fires to put out.

But this picture in Ezra 6:22 is so different. It is so assuring to read that anxiety is not the thing swirling around God's people in the middle of this celebration. Instead, God's favor and joy are in their midst. *He made them joyful*, it says.

Why were they joyful? They were joyful because God delivered them from their former exile in Babylon, and they were now free to return to their own land. More than that, they were joyful that God was allowing them to finally rebuild God's temple, a central place of worship for them, where they got to access God's presence. On top of that, the very empire that punished them hundreds of years before, was now being used by God to help them build this temple! God had turned things around and answered their prayers!

To commemorate this, they celebrated for seven days. A long party indeed! The number seven is a biblical symbol of wholeness, completeness, or totality, which means this seven-day party should give us the impression of "continual joy."

What makes you this joyful?

I know it feels good when things go our way or when God shows favor over us. We can feel so relieved when we see our prayers answered. How do you typically respond to those moments?

In seasons of plenty or times of refreshment, we can respond in a number of ways. Sometimes we can get used to our situation and simply forget we're in the "good times" to begin with! We can grow apathetic and ungrateful. Other times, we know we're in a season of good times, but we mistakenly take the credit for it, thinking we got ourselves there all on our own. We feel "good vibes," but it's not quite the same thing as God making us joyful.

Let us not take credit for the good season, friend. For God is the one in control. He holds all wisdom and power to move our circumstances in various directions. We don't have that kind of power, even when we try! Let us not feel happy for a little while, for a few fleeting seconds, and then move on in forgetfulness. Instead, let us live in joy—the *seven-day* kind of joy—because God lives in us!

How, then, do we not take credit for our blessings? What helps us remember that it is *God's* kind hand at work in the good times? What helps us develop godly joy in those seasons? Thankfulness.

Can you believe I didn't know "thank-you notes" were a thing? I grew up outside of America in my younger years, so after my bridal shower, my favorite classy hostess told me it was a must. This was just the way it worked here. Without her reminder, I would have forgotten to make a thank-you note to my party guests for the gifts! So I spent a week writing thank-you letters.

Let me ask you a question: Have you forgotten to thank God? Would your lack of thankfulness communicate to Him that you are a foreigner to the ways of heaven? If you have forgotten, remember you can thank Him anytime and anywhere. Take a minute and thank Him for anything and everything, for the air we breathe right now. For Christ, who satisfied our debt. Don't forget every day is a gift. Don't forget to bless the name of the Lord and glorify Him in moments of great honor or happiness (Luke 1:46–47).

God doesn't want you to fly right by the good seasons in this life. No, He wants you to stop and find *joy* in them. His joy! *Seven-day* joy that keeps going as you pour out thankfulness to Him.

How has God answered your prayers? How has He shown up? Where have you seen His hand at work? What evidence of His mighty hand do you see? Stop and thank Him. Instead of being apathetic or forgetful or stealing credit, let Him make you joyful! Evidence of His gifts and His sovereign hand shows up in our life every day, so go looking for it. And sister, *write that thank-you note.*

PRAYER: Oh Father, thank You for the gifts in the good seasons! I so often forget to stop and give You praise for moments of happiness or prayers answered. I pray and rejoice right now in the greatest gift—the name of Your Son Jesus. Thank You for being my refuge and my joy in every season. When I take credit for good circumstances, convict me and help me remember You are the giver of all good things. I stop right now to say "My soul glorifies the Lord and my spirit rejoices in God my Savior" (Luke 1:46–47 NIV). Give me eyes to recognize Your mighty hand over my life and to rejoice in Your holy name when I see You move on my behalf. Through Your Spirit, give me the seven-day kind of joy, Father! In Jesus's name, Amen.

REFLECTION QUESTIONS

To experience joy, we have to overcome the temptation toward apathy, forgetfulness, or stealing credit. When it comes to experiencing godly joy in the good times, which of these three things is your primary struggle?

Think back over your life. Which seasons would you classify as the "good times"? How did God orchestrate those seasons to happen?

_____

_____

_____

_____

Read Psalm 31:19. Who are the "good things" especially bestowed upon? What does this challenge you to do?

_____

_____

_____

_____

_____

_____

_____

_____

_____

_____

_____

_____

_____

_____

_____

_____

_____

_____

_____

_____

Read Psalm 16:11 and then Psalm 13:6. Where can we go to be most filled with joy (16:11)? What should be our response (13:6)?

_____

_____

_____

_____

JOY IN THE
BAD SEASONS

JOY // DAY 4

May the God of hope fill you with all joy and peace in believing,
so that by the power of the Holy Spirit you may abound in hope.

ROMANS 15:13 (ESV)

"Life could have been much different if I had not gone through difficulties, challenges, and pain."

For a lot of my life, I would have said that statement in a negative way. I would have dreamed about the life I could have had, absent from the struggles. The picture-perfect life would flash before my eyes, and I'd feel sad about the ways my life didn't line up with it.

But now I say that statement in a totally new way. If it weren't for the dark seasons, I don't believe I would be the person I am today. Life would certainly be different—meaning that the woman living that life would definitely not have had the strength of God that resides in me today. That other version of me, well, she would have never learned to trust the Lord the way I do now, even when I cannot see the outcome. She wouldn't hear that constant voice of the Spirit in her saying, "TRUST ME." She wouldn't have learned to trust the reminders from God that I don't need to fix it, or grasp for control in the situation, or act in my own strength when I clearly can't do it alone. If that life was the one God actually gave me, I wouldn't be a person who, by the grace of God, fights to surrender to what is about to happen in the Lord.

This is what happens when God fills us with joy during the bad seasons—it helps us see things from a different perspective. Instead of thinking, *Oh no! The rainy season is here. God is clearly out to get me!* the

Spirit's joy in us allows us to think instead, *Maybe the rain is here to help me grow up taller and stronger than if the rain had never come.*

With joy in our hearts produced by the Holy Spirit, we can now even think this way: *Perhaps this bad season in life is to help someone in the future and encourage them in a way nobody else can.* Or as Paul would put it, because of the joy we have, we can say this of our troubling moments: "Praise be to the God and Father of our Lord Jesus Christ, the Father of compassion and the God of all comfort, who comforts us in all our troubles, so that we can comfort those in any trouble with the comfort we ourselves receive from God" (2 Cor. 1:3–4 NIV).

So how can we be filled with this joy from God in the hard seasons? Our first action is *prayer*—asking the Lord for help. The next step is to *surrender* whatever it is we are holding back. (Chances are, that is the thing usually holding us back from growth!) If you don't know what to surrender, ask the Lord! The Holy Spirit will answer that prayer if there is something you are holding onto. He will reveal it to you and even help you let go of it at the end of your prayer!

We have no power on our own, but we do know the one who holds all of it. So let's ask Him to give us strength to bear any bad season with joy.

I probably made it sound like it is an easy process, but it isn't. For me, it has taken many failures to learn what joy looks like in the dark valleys. As I've practiced these things, though, I've learned to forgive those who made the journey hard and even thank God for them because if it was not for them, I would have never learned to be more like Jesus, who loved me, His former enemy. Without them, I would have never learned from their mistakes or mine. Without those hard seasons, I would have missed out on God's overall plan for me, because sometimes, the dark paths paved the way toward the bright ones!

Life is hard. There's no question about that. But life can be really *different* right in the middle of the hard and the struggle, if we ask God to fill us up with His joy.

According to 1 Peter 1:8–9 (NIV), it really is possible to be "filled with an inexpressible and glorious joy." And remember, Peter writes this not to those who are rolling through life on Easy Street, but to those who are suffering and struggling! He doesn't say this is possible if you are living the good life. He says this is true if "you believe in him." Meaning, this kind of joy is reserved for you only if you are a believer. And so, it means this joy is possible for *any* Christian at *any* time. Why? Because our joy is found in Christ's life, death, and resurrection. We rejoice not in our circumstances, but in our salvation, which is always something to be joyful about! We have nothing to lose because we have it all already—help for right now, and a resurrection life later!

Yes, I know, you might be thinking, *Well I lost a loved one* or *I lost a marriage* or *I lost a job.* Maybe you are going through a lot right now. Maybe you're lonely, single, childless, or facing a bank account that gets lower by the day. First, let me say this: your pain is *real* and God wants to meet you in it. He does not want you to act like nothing is wrong. He draws near to you in your pain and comforts you! Second, let me say this: deep, abiding, pure joy is possible, *even there*. That kind of joy doesn't require having the perfect job, the perfect marriage, or the perfect family. Nor does it require having *any* job, marriage, or family. God's joy can give you perspective on the meaning of life above all those things you desire, and it can give you endurance through the loss of those things too.

God is forming you into the person He wants you to be. And the life He gave you, including the hard seasons, is the path He forged for you to get there. The rainy moments on that path are what help us discover the strength and experience the joy that will build us up to be that person God has made us to be. Yes, we all have a purpose (and sometimes it is right in front of you!), and His joy is the only thing strong enough to get us through anything we can face. In hard times, we need to remind ourselves over again that the joy God offers is the joy of *salvation*. And nothing can take that away from us. In the face of so many lesser places to run for power and help, we must resolve to choose the best form of help, saying to God, "the joy of the LORD is [my] strength" and "restore the joy of your salvation to me" in the hard times! (Nch. 8:10; Ps. 51:12).

It's so beautiful to know that Jesus has given us inexpressible joy even in the pain. Let's lean into it together, friend. No matter how hard the rain pours.

PRAYER: Heavenly Father, I run to You right now in the pain. I surrender in obedience, ready to receive Your joy that will give me the strength and the power I need. Only You can give me the ability to endure this hard season with deep and abiding joy. You have a will for my life—a person You are shaping me into. A person who looks like Christ! I give You the dark circumstances in my life right now, and ask that You use it to shape me into that person and fulfill Your will in my life. When I forget, please remind me that Your everlasting joy is possible, even here. Help me trust You when it is hard, that this pain is temporary and not eternal. Help me find joy in what is eternal—the life and power You give me in Your salvation! My soul is saved and my future in the resurrection is secure, thanks to You. Allow this truth to crown my head in gladness and give me everlasting joy (Isa. 35:10)! In Jesus's name, Amen..

REFLECTION QUESTIONS

Looking back on your life, what challenge do you see more clearly now as something God was using to make you into the person you are now? Have you thanked Him for using that situation for your good? If not, it is never too late to lift it up in prayer.

What is the greatest challenge or dark situation that you face today? Do you think deep, inexpressible joy is a possibility in this season? Why or why not?

Where do you typically run for joy when you face a dark or rainy season? How has that thing failed to give you lasting joy in the past? Why do you keep running to it?

_____

_____

_____

_____

_____

_____

_____

_____

_____

_____

_____

_____

_____

_____

_____

_____

_____

_____

_____

_____

_____

_____

_____

_____

_____

_____

What makes God's joy different than worldly joy? When was the last time you deeply rejoiced in your salvation? Take some time to do that now.

REJOICING ALWAYS

JOY // DAY 5

Rejoice in the Lord always; again I will say, rejoice.
Let your reasonableness be known to everyone.

PHILIPPIANS 4:4–5 (ESV)

As we've explored before, biblical joy is all about perspective. Without that perspective, we will find this command to *always* rejoice a pretty hard command to follow. And it is hard to follow if you define joy by how you are doing at the moment. But what if you defined it by what God has done in your life? By what He did for you in salvation? By what His character is like? What if you resolved to believe what the Bible says—that joy is found in *the Lord*?

As a follower of Christ, no matter our circumstances, it is always possible to rejoice in the Lord. When we look at our verse for today, we must remember that Paul wrote this to a church from prison. If anyone had a reason not to write down this verse, it was Paul. And yet he clearly encouraged the church to rejoice always.

Paul was living in joy in prison, and Jesus did the same on the cross. Can you live in joy from your current circumstances? Keep your eyes on Jesus. If He can bear the cross with joy, and His servant Paul can bear prison in joy too, what does that tell you about your current problems? They are no match for God's joy! They are no threat to God's Spirit who lives inside you and wants to bear the fruit of joy in your heart! Friend, our feelings are just not strong enough to rewrite the Lord's great joy. We will not find joy in the world but in the Holy Spirit who enables us to see farther than our circumstances.

What if you shifted your joy from your current problems to the things Jesus has already given you? Would that help you? It would certainly help me! I know this is challenging—especially when it's hard, but what if instead of looking for how the current problem could be fixed, we asked God to use it—however it turns out—for His glory either way?

I love that this verse puts "reasonable" right next to rejoicing. After all, after a long stretch of joylessness in our lives, we start getting pretty unreasonable, don't we? In our lack of joy over what God has given us, or how He has sustained us, we start comparing to everyone else, and then we march in God's throne room, demanding our lives look a certain way in order to be okay. We start believing other people's lives would give us the joy we want, and like a bratty kid at Christmas, out come all our unreasonable standards and requests.

I struggled with this back in the high school years. I remember thinking, *Why is my life so different from my friends'?* I had to go home to my parents arguing, or an empty fridge, or to a final notice to pay our rent. I had to face a father who left us and, later, my parents' divorce. We even became homeless—I lived with a family member for some time. I still carry that comparison struggle into my life as an adult. I still get stuck in the mentality that everyone else seems to be living their best life. Back in high school and even now, I can get so caught up on my circumstances that my joy becomes nonexistent, eaten up by comparison and discontentment.

Now, hear me out: calling out to God in seasons of hunger or parentlessness is not a bad thing, of course. My wounds were valid back then, just as they are now. And God *wants* us to come to Him with that stuff. The difference is, what now makes me okay inside is *God's* joy and provision and care, not a perfect set of circumstances. Because of the Holy Spirit, my joy is found in getting *God's* life inside of me, *not getting someone else's life*. After learning that God could meet me in my wounded places, and even provide for me in miraculous ways (He kept me fed, and I thank Him for giving me a safe place to live with those family members!), I realized that joy was keeping me grounded. It was helping me endure without becoming bitter. I learned that a heart that rejoices is one that can be reasonable with God, with themselves, and with their neighbors. Again, God's joy gives *proper perspective*. That makes us reasonable, thankful people instead of cranky and demanding!

In the lack of contentment in the Lord, you will find no fruit of joy in your life, but when you find your delight in Christ, you will experience the contentment that Paul is talking about in this passage. Most of us are free citizens on the outside, but prisoners to discontentment on the inside. But Paul—he was a prisoner on the outside, and yet He was set free in joy on the inside. You can be too.

You know what else God's joy does for the person who leans into it often? It lets you feel joy for those who are having a good season. You have the power to be genuinely happy for them instead of jealous. You can rejoice together!

Some people are coming out of tribulations when others are entering, and some are in between storms. *Rejoice always* means that you rejoice with those people too. You help them remember all the ways God has helped them in the past so they might trust Him right now. When they are weak or tempted to forget, you remind them God is for them and not against them. You can't do that for others if you aren't walking in the joy yourself! This is another reason we must *rejoice always*; our friends in the storm need it!

Rejoicing always means "at all times." At all occasions, consistently, without fail, regularly, repeatedly, constantly. Many of us feel resistance here, don't we? *But I'm not a consistent person in anything*, you might say. I'm willing to wager that's not entirely true. Think about it. We can be consistent in many ways throughout our lives. My husband *knows* I am consistent in my shopping habits. (Maybe I'm not alone there?) My bank account will tell you I'm consistent in my eating-out habits. (Anybody else?) My phone will tell you I'm consistent in my social media or enter-tainment habits. (Okay, I *know* I got you there! This one is true for all of us!) The reality is that believers do plenty of things on the regular. Rejoicing is most certainly possible! So, together, let's uncross our arms and give this thing called rejoicing a shot. Let's come together in one agreement so we can see our joy complete.

Rejoice in every season, friend. Good or bad, rejoice always. For He is using everything for His good, and you are part of it. Life is better living in His joy than without it. Take hold of the joy offered to you in your salvation. Our Savior is coming. In the meantime, between now and then, remember that rejoicing always keeps you reasonable. It keeps you thank-ful. It allows you to celebrate with those you once hated, and it empowers you to walk others through their storms. Rejoice always!

PRAYER: Oh Lord, I ask that You shower me with Your joy in every season of my life, pleasant or unpleasant. I pray that You help me practice Your command of rejoicing always, even in the places I feel like it's not possible. Thank You for reminding me there is nothing that can separate me from Your joy and that You are always with me. Even in the fire, You are with me. Rain or shine! Help me be consistent in joy, so that I might not only be joyful, but reasonable, and able to rejoice with those on the mountaintop and help those walking through the valley! Complete in me the joy You have promised to bear in me through Your Spirit. In Jesus's name, Amen.

REFLECTION QUESTIONS

Explain how joy is related to proper perspective in your own words.

How have you seen God's joy help you in moments of comparison?

Fill in the blank here: "I've been waiting on _____ to happen before I'll rejoice in all circumstances." Why have you been waiting on this? Is that something the Bible says you have to wait on before you can rejoice? How does Paul's example help you?

Rejoicing always helps us be reasonable, it helps us celebrate those who are experiencing good things, and it helps us walk others through the storm. Which of these three things do you struggle with most? Have you ever related this struggle with your lack of consistent rejoicing?

REFLECTION AND REST

Use the last two days of this week to rest from reading, and instead, reflect on what you've learned. Use the journaling prompts and space below to process and enjoy what the Lord is doing in your heart.

1. What aspect of God's joy did you find most encouraging this week? Most surprising?

_____

_____

_____

_____

_____

_____

_____

2. In what tangible ways do you see the fruit of joy being developed by God's Spirit in your heart and actions? Take some time to thank God for this fruitful work He's doing in you.

_____

_____

_____

_____

_____

_____

_____

_____

_____

_____

3. In this season of your life, which of these needs the most development in your heart? Circle one.

Joy in the Good Seasons.   Joy in the Bad Seasons.   Rejoicing Always.

What are some practical next steps you can take to develop this?

_____

_____

_____

_____

_____

_____

_____

_____

_____

_____

FREESTYLE REFLECTION

Use this space below to pray, write out a meaningful passage of Scripture, or process anything God has placed on your heart this week.

GOD OUR PEACEMAKER

PEACE // DAY 1

Remember that you were at that time separated from Christ, alienated from the commonwealth of Israel and strangers to the covenants of promise, having no hope and without God in the world. But now in Christ Jesus you who once were far off have been brought near by the blood of Christ. For he himself is our peace, who has made us both one and has broken down in his flesh the dividing wall of hostility by abolishing the law of commandments expressed in ordinances, that he might create in himself one new man in place of the two, so making peace, and might reconcile us both to God in one body through the cross, thereby killing the hostility. And he came and preached peace to you who were far off and peace to those who were near. For through him we both have access in one Spirit to the Father. So then you are no longer strangers and aliens, but you are fellow citizens with the saints and members of the household of God, built on the foundation of the apostles and prophets, Christ Jesus himself being the cornerstone. . . .

For in him all the fullness of God was pleased to dwell, and through him to reconcile to himself all things, whether on earth or in heaven, making peace by the blood of his cross.

EPHESIANS 2:12–20; COLOSSIANS 1:19–20 (ESV)

Who doesn't want a little more peace in her life? Whether it's the wars going on in our world or the ones going on inside our own hearts, who doesn't want to feel at rest instead of constantly at battle?

Oftentimes, we forget that our desire for a state of peace doesn't actually originate in us. It originates in God. Our God is a God of peace, and since we are made in His image, we naturally ache for peace too.

But God knew. God knew what I had seen and what my family was going through. So he did what Romans 5:8 tells us about God: he didn't merely *feel* love for my family, he *demonstrated* that love by sending someone to us to help in a time of need.

How does God show He's a God of peace? Well, we could start by looking at the way He made the world. When He first speaks creation into existence, He makes a world that is in total harmony with itself (and with Him). He doesn't create the elements—like water and earth and wind—in a way that puts them at war with one another, but rather working together to create a beautiful ecosystem. And when He first makes humankind, we notice they, too, are not at war with one another. Their natural state is peace. This is the kind of world God always wanted.

The wars came along when sin came along. And when sin entered the world, for the first time ever, it put humankind and God on opposite sides instead of the same side. Where there used to be harmonious, intimate relationship between humankind and God, sin separated the two, making them enemies. And the separation isn't small, like two sides of a creek bed. No, it's bigger than an ocean. We, stuck over here, and Him, over there on the other side of the chasm.

Since the day that sin entered the world, the Bible says we are strangers to God, born apart from the Lord. Everything changed. And this separation between a Holy God and sin makes sense. A holy God cannot be part of sin, meaning sin and holiness cannot live side by side. The barrier was established, and we were separated from God and His righteousness. More than that, wrath was stored up for all of us on this side of the divide. Sin and wrongdoing—it has to be accounted for. And so there we sit, far away from God as His enemy, waiting on the day we answer for all we've done wrong.

You'd think we'd be stuck in this sad situation forever. But remember—God is a God of peace. Peace with His children and a world at peace with itself is what He has always wanted! And so He looked at the war— the separation between us and Him—and He made a way to achieve that peace once and for all.

The Lord built what I like to call a "bridge plan," strong enough to take on the wrath to save us and reconcile us back to Himself. The reconciliation had a hefty price tag. Only the blood shed by Jesus Christ, the Son of God, could bring us back to the Father. When He came to earth, Jesus became flesh—human like you and me—so that He might become our mediator, negotiator, conciliator, middleman, and intercessor between His Father and us. And when He endured the cross, He paid the debt for all our sin and wrongdoing so that we might no longer have a separation between ourselves and God. He is our Peacemaker because His blood brought us near the Father (Eph. 2:13).

Rejoice in this today, friend: His sacrifice did pay it all! We have been reconciled back to God Himself through Christ! Christ's cross proves our God is a lover of peace and will go to great lengths to end our war with Him, putting things back together the way they were always supposed to be. It proves that God desires no person be a stranger to Him, but rather be close to Him in love.

Do you remember when you were a "stranger" or "foreigner" to God? Do you remember the time before you were brought near? Growing up as an immigrant, it is wild how much I can relate to this language in the Bible. A stranger, a foreigner, a Gentile. A Gentile was morally separated from God and also relationally separated from God's chosen people, the Jews. Thinking back on my childhood, I remember the sting of what that felt like. I remember what it was like to be an outcast. I was different from the kids I went to school with: I dressed differently, I talked differently. No matter how hard I tried to fit in, I didn't.

But you know what? I knew I had something that some of them did not, which was Jesus, my peace, my family, my strength, and hope. I thank God He didn't alienate me. No matter how hard it got, I knew I had been brought near to my heavenly Father through the precious blood of the Savior. Yeah, I felt different—I still do, even as a full-fledged citizen of the U.S. My days might have been full of strife or people misunderstanding me (or even making fun of me), but nothing could take away the fact that God had made peace with me—I was His!

Have you ever traveled in a country you found beautiful, and wondered what it would be like to live there for real? Getting citizenship in a new country is interesting. I know from experience! You can become a citizen, and that's great. But here's the truth: that process can reconcile you to a country's government but not necessarily to the people. The blood of Christ, however, is different. It gives us citizenship into the family of God. It reconciles us to God the Father and also to His people. Isn't that amazing? God makes peace not just between believers and Himself, but believers with one another, since they are all His kingdom citizens!

Here's the gospel: before Christ, we were all outsiders. We were all foreigners to the kingdom of God! If Gentiles, we weren't His chosen people. But you know what? We didn't have to become Jews to become part of the family. We just had to believe in Him, and what His shed blood accomplished on our behalf, so that we might all become one big family.

Jesus did that for us. He united us. He is both our peace and peacemaker. He restored us and connected us, and we are now one body in Christ. We are His church, and we work together in unity. At the cross, everything that caused our separation was destroyed!

How great it is to know that our God is a Peacemaker. That He'd go as far as the cross to set things right again between us and Him (and one another!), and that He will one day come and finish the job in whole, setting the entire world right again, at peace, just as it should be. As you move forward this week, asking the Spirit to bear more peace in your life, allow this truth to sweep over you: the Spirit bears peace in you because your God is full of it—and He proved that on the cross!

PRAYER: Oh Jesus, thank You for being my peacemaker! You became the mediator that I needed. Only You could have reestablished my relationship with the Father. Lord, I am so grateful for Your blood that paid it all—for taking the wrath I deserved, and making me a child of God instead of an enemy! Instead of letting me stay a stranger and foreigner to Your household, thank You for making me a part of Your family, the church! No matter how out of place I feel in this world, I will always belong to You and Your people—I am so grateful. There is much war in this world; thank You for being a God of peace in the midst of it! I ask that Your Spirit would make me more like You in this way—a peacemaker. In Your precious name, Amen.

REFLECTION QUESTIONS

When you think of all God's character traits, is peace something you consider a primary trait? Why or why not?

Whether you were traveling to another country or hanging out with a group of people who were different from you, have you ever found yourself the "odd man out"? How did that alienation feel? How did you handle it?

_____

_____

_____

What are some things our culture trusts in to make peace between two warring parties?

_____

_____

_____

_____

_____

_____

_____

_____

_____

_____

_____

_____

_____

_____

_____

_____

_____

_____

_____

_____

Explain in your own words, why the blood of Christ shed on the cross is the only thing that can make peace between us and God, and between us and each other.

_____

_____

_____

_____

_____

A DIFFERENT
KIND OF PIECE

PEACE // DAY 2

"Peace I leave with you. My peace I give to you. I do not give to you
as the world gives. Don't let your hearts be troubled or fearful."

JOHN 14:27

When you were a child, where did you go to find peace when your world
felt chaotic?

Growing up in a hostile environment, peace was tough to find for me. I
had to find it outside my home and family, which meant that I needed to go
outside most of the time. If I was home, it meant spending many hours in
my room. I say "my room," but the truth is, most of the time I had to share
my room with my siblings. And so getting any alone time in that sacred
spot was rare.

Eventually, I found peace in long runs and in school. I'd always show
up early to before-school practices and stay late when after-school track (or
cross-country) practice was over. I tried to keep myself busy, and running
gave me peace and a safe place. I'm grateful to God for it; it was a gift. But
at the same time, it was just a temporary type of peace. Eventually, after
my workouts during the day, I had to face the reality of things at home. My
relief didn't last for long, and after some time passed, I realized the things
of this world would never fulfill me in a permanent way.

The tricky part was trying to figure out what would.

I knew that drugs wouldn't give me peace just by looking at my dad. I
knew that bouncing around between a bunch of boys wouldn't either, this
time by looking at my mom's life. And so I tried to find love and peace in
just *one* boy. But that approach to peace turned out badly too. The relationship turned violent, and I ended up stuck in it for almost four years.

What's your story when it comes to finding peace in this life? You likely already know where you went to find it as a child. I wonder—where do you try to find it now? Does it last?

Whatever your answer is, here's some good news: the kind of peace Jesus offers is better than any worldly version. In John 14:27, we see that Jesus has left us a rich and abundant inheritance of peace. It's a heavenly peace only believers can claim. The kind of peace only He can provide. It does not come from our outer circumstances—the family being put together or the boy liking us or the house being clean. It is inward peace, one that bubbles up from down deep, because He lives in us. His peace is different, unlike the worldly version that only lasts temporarily. Jesus's peace is not temporary. It's *abiding*. No matter what is going on in our life—crazy family or otherwise—it sticks around. We don't have to be afraid to lose it every second. It's not going anywhere.

Peace like this only He can give to those who are in the right relationship with God—those who have trusted Christ, and therefore know their assurance of His forgiveness and have enjoyed full reconciliation with the Father. When this is true of a person, God's Spirit indwells them, and His peace keeps pouring out like living water within them. Isn't that amazing? Just like His love and His joy, God's peace won't ever stop flowing out of Him, into you! Once I realized this in my own pursuit of peace, I realized I didn't need the perfect family or the boyfriend—I had all the peace I needed, provided by God Himself!

I love the comfort the last sentence of this verse brings to us: "Let not your hearts be troubled, neither let them be afraid" (ESV). Jesus is making a clear promise we might miss at first glance, but it is there because God knows we need the reminder of what His peace has the power to do for us. It can soothe our troubles and our fears. It can overcome them with surpassing, heavenly peace this world knows nothing of. His peace is different. It works in us to such a level that our hearts are no longer held captive by trouble and fear.

What do you do when you are worried and afraid (Ps. 56:11)? Do you run toward this promise? Do you ask Jesus to help the Spirit's peace dwell in your heart? Because it's there, deep down. It abides in you!

The enemy will try anything to steal and destroy your peace. He hates the fruit in our lives, and longs to pluck it and make it look like God's vine is empty! Has the enemy tried to do this to you? Has he tried to take your peace? Most likely. And that makes sense. He is good at that. But we have to resist him, and he will flee from us (James 4:7). When it comes to fruit, the enemy is all about taking away, and God is about giving and giving some more. So trust Him to keep cultivating peace in your heart. He will! And nobody can take anything away provided by the Lord!

Isn't that good news today? Love starts with God because He loved us first. He loved you before you loved Him. He has given Himself to you. And that makes all the difference when it comes to bearing the fruit of love in our own lives. We can't bear any fruit of love toward others until we understand just how much He loves us. Will you trust in that love today?

Knowing all this about Jesus's peace can help us fight against our internal war against sin, fear, doubt, and many other struggles. Knowing this has helped me, and I hope it enables you to win the war within yourself. Friend, His peace restrains any power that can hinder us and it sets us free from the paralysis of fear. The hard things may still be true in our lives, but Jesus's peace gives us the power to stop cowering or freezing in fear, and *walk* amidst them freely.

Running and relationships—those offered me temporary peace. But they didn't help me walk free of fear. Only Jesus's peace can do that. Let's trust Him for that today!

PRAYER: Oh Lord, thank You for the assurances and promises You give us in Your Word, especially this one about Your peace! You know the ways I try to find peace in this life. I thank You for the ways some of those things may help in temporary ways, but I come to You right now and ask that through Your Spirit, You'll cultivate something even better and more lasting in my heart—Jesus's peace. You also know the things I run to for peace that are not healthy, and I stop right now and surrender that to You, confessing it has failed me in ways You could never fail me! I bring You all my troubles today, and the things I am afraid of—You know them each by name. I pray that Your peace would flood my heart, even now, helping me overcome the fear and walk freely through my situation. In Jesus's name, Amen.

REFLECTION QUESTIONS

What is your current "go to" when you feel fear, trouble, or chaos?

_____

_____

_____

_____

_____

_____

_____

_____

_____

_____

_____

_____

_____

_____

_____

_____

_____

_____

_____

_____

_____

_____

_____

_____

_____

_____

_____

_____

_____

_____

_____

_____

In what ways does that thing offer you temporary peace? In what ways has it failed you?

_____

_____

_____

Why is Jesus's peace better?

_____

_____

_____

_____

_____

_____

_____

_____

_____

_____

_____

_____

_____

_____

_____

_____

_____

_____

_____

_____

_____

_____

_____

_____

_____

_____

In what ways is the enemy trying to steal your Spirit-given peace? What are some practical things you can do to resist him?

_____

_____

_____

_____

PEACE WITH OTHERS

PEACE // DAY 3

Strive for peace with everyone.

HEBREWS 12:14 (ESV)

"Strive for peace with everyone." Whew. That sounds impossible on a large scale, doesn't it? How can we possibly ensure *everyone* feels at peace with us? What about those who, despite our best intentions at being a witness for Christ, hate us? What about those who, despite our efforts to restore the relationship after a disagreement, stubbornly refuse to reconcile with us? What about our little kids who, despite all we've done to calm the tantrum and provide soothing relief, still stomp around and cry about not getting their way?

Here's the good news: the challenge for everyone in the world to feel at peace with us is not what this Scripture is trying to communicate. Instead, it challenges the other way around. It is asking *us* to pursue peace with *them*. After all, the only person we can change is ourselves. This Scripture, along with every other passage in the Bible, trains us for every good work. To do that, the Bible doesn't point toward everybody else to tell them to get in line. It points at *us*, helping *us* deal with *our own* hearts before the Lord, cleansing us from what is going wrong inside of us so we might "be instruments for special purposes, made holy, useful to the Master and prepared to do any good work" (2 Tim. 2:21 NIV). It pushes us not to outward modification, but to inward change. That is what happens to a heart that is reading and applying the Scriptures.

As the Spirit bears the fruit of peace within us as Christians, that peace naturally flows outward. And so, as far as it depends on us, we strive for peace in every relationship—with everyone, all the time. If we claim to have God's peace in us, then our lives should show it, and we should settle any tension in our relationships and bring peace to any problem that is not settled.

How do you usually handle an unsettled relationship? In my case, I tend to just cut off communication entirely, and stay out of the way, so the conflict can stay swept under the rug and I don't have to deal with it. Have you ever done that? It seems like such an easy solution. Yet that is not the work of striving for peace. Sometimes peace has to be *made*. It requires effort and intentionality. Ignoring the conflict is not really peace—it's false peace. It's acting like you're in a peaceful place with someone when the truth is, you are not! My neglect to strive for peace, even when it is uncomfortable, is still sin and is a problem.

Instead of that, what if we dealt with what we held against someone else? Friend, the relationships in our lives are a gift. Let's not have anything against one another that would take away the peace between one another. Having anything against each other—especially if we let it fester and we choose not to approach our sister or brother about it directly—is a sin, as love "does not keep a record of wrongs" (1 Cor. 13:5). Peace should be a life-giving rain that showers down on everything in our home, in our relationships, our marriages, our friendships, our family, and our church community.

In what relationships do you tend to harbor the most anger or bitterness? What situations do you allow conflict to stew in your heart? For example, very often I receive emails or messages about one particular environment—the church. I get asked how to deal with people at the church who will often make a woman feel unwanted and excluded. Has that ever happened to you?

What a hard situation. Surely it is much easier to express love and peace with the people in our life who have proven themselves friends. They know us. They get us. They love us. And the Bible does call us to love them well and pursue peace with them. But it also calls us beyond them—to "everyone." Even those people, for example, who we barely know in some Bible study group we didn't handpick ourselves—you know, the ones that interrupt us all the time or fail to see our gifts. In this example, here's perspective that can keep us pursuing peace: maybe we didn't handpick the situation for ourselves, but God did. And He did for a reason.

The first thing we must ask ourselves in challenging relationships is this: What is this relationship *for*, after all? What's the point of it? For me to feel catered to and prioritized every minute? For me to receive accolades and applause and approval? Is that the big point of all relationships? Is that the whole reason for the church?

We know the answer: No. We go to church (or Bible study) to worship a holy God. And the relationships in our lives are there to grow us in all sorts of ways, one of those ways being *learning how to be a peacemaker like Jesus*. Without those hard relationships, what else would teach us to do this? Most encouraging in all of this is that although they might not see what you see, God is working on them too. They need to learn what striving for peace looks like in their own spiritual development, and perhaps God crossed your paths to show you what that looks like—to show you a living example of what He went through to make peace with you.

Friend, believers should love one another as neighbors and like brothers and sisters, as we are God's children. I sure know it's hard to strive for peace when the other party has real issues to work through. I've been there! Here's what I've learned: let God work on them and look inside your own heart. You may be surprised to find that the sin within is the same sin you see in them—that thing that gets on your nerves! Many times, the things we get most upset about in other people are like a mirror—they reflect our own inner problems. Regardless of what you find when you look inside your heart, know that God will take care of the stuff going on in the other side of the relationship. He can handle them. Just bring Him what you're dealing with, and after you do, strive for peace with your neighbor.

Who in your life is good at this? Get around them, and watch their ways. For me, this is my husband. I admire the way he makes peace with everyone in his workspace and his family, which is not easy! In our relationship, he is the peacemaker in our home. He knows the hard time I have when it comes to getting along with my mother, and he constantly reminds me to make peace with her, even if we have different points of view. Who is that person for you? Who can help you "pursue what promotes peace and what builds up one another" (Rom. 14:19)? Go get some time around them! And remember, no matter how hard it gets, Jesus is your guide. He shows you how to make peace, even when it's hard. Think on this as you walk forward today: How did Jesus make peace between you and God? And what would it look like for you to follow in His footsteps today, even in the hardest of relationships?

> "Blessed are the peacemakers,
> for they will be called sons of God."
>
> (Matt. 5:9)

PRAYER: Oh Jesus, thank You for Your example of peacemaking. In it, You show me what it means to make peace with those who I'm at odds with! I humble myself to serve You and to worship You and mimic You in this way. Please search my heart for any records I may be keeping against those I am supposed to be making peace with. Help me strive for peace and mutual up-lifting, even when it is hard. Bring to mind the people I need to have a direct conversation with—help me trust You with what is happening on their side of the relationship, and give me the strength to look inside my own heart for any sin that may be there. Cleanse me within, and set me apart as an instrument for Your holy and useful work! Make me more like You, a peacemaker and kind friend. In Jesus's name, Amen.

REFLECTION QUESTIONS

What do you strive most for on any given day?

Consider the thing you wrote above. What would be different about your life if you were to strive for biblical peace as much as you strive for that thing?

**Who do you need to
make peace with
right now?**

**What unsettled
relationships
need settling?**

PEACE THAT GUARDS

PEACE // DAY 4

Do not be anxious about anything, but in everything by prayer and supplication with thanksgiving let your requests be made known to God. And the peace of God, which surpasses all understanding, will guard your hearts and your minds in Christ Jesus.

PHILIPPIANS 4:6–7 (ESV)

If you could personify peace, what kind of person would it look like? Many of us might immediately picture someone who soothes others—maybe the parent of a little one, whispering reassuring words into the ear of their crying child in the middle of the night and lightly scratching their back until the nightmare goes away. Or perhaps we picture someone like a massage therapist who eases away our tension, speaking quietly to us in a dimly lit room filled with the aroma of essential oils.

But Paul uses a different word here in Philippians. He doesn't say peace soothes or whispers to our hearts. He says peace *guards* our hearts.

When was the last time a *guard* was your mental image of peace? It's a totally different picture than what we might expect, right? Instead of tranquil or passive or easy-breezy or relaxed, we see something strong, armed, and ready to defend against attack. Alert. Protective.

A guard is someone you don't mess with. And apparently, so is God's peace! It has the power to ward off intruders and defend against attacks.

What kind of attacks, you might ask? All sorts of kinds, I'm sure, but this verse seems to narrow in on *anxiety* in particular.

Anxiety. What a cruel captor. It creeps up and takes us hostage, usually because we are stressed about some sort of circumstance we can't control. At the bottom of things, we know the truth—we can't control all the evil or sin in the world. And yet we still worry, sometimes to the point of debilitation.

So what can we do in those moments? Instead of worrying about the things we can't control, we can choose to focus on two things: (1) what's going on in our own hearts and minds and (2) what we need to bring to God and *leave with Him*. When we do this—when we go to God and pray about our worries and our problems, thanking Him for His help and making our requests clear—God's peace will flood us. It will coat and cover over our hearts, all the way around, like a shield. When we go to God and throw all our anxieties on Him, and we can trust that He will take care of the rest, just like He always has. And no matter how bad it gets, we can always remember we have assurance in our salvation—that Jesus's work on the cross covers our sin and our debt, and that His resurrection promises us eternal life. Even if the world as we know it really does fall apart, even if it *ends*, we get to live in the world that is coming—in God's future heaven-on-earth.

Nothing can give you peace like that, and nothing can take that future hope away from you! So run to the Lord, friend, and watch as He guards your heart and mind with His peace. When you feel anxious or afraid, run to the sword of God's Word and the shield of His peace—for they have the power to fight for you!

We know who our God is—the Lord of Peace. And when we run to Him with our troubles and scary moments, we can trust that He will prove Himself as our guard, our shield, our protector, our defender. He will look after us because He cares for us.

Guard your heart in prayer every day and at all times, friend. This will keep you in what I like to call a "prayer bubble." This "bubble" keeps you in constant communication and conversation with God. I live in the bubble! Even my kids find me speaking out loud sometimes, and they ask me, "Mom, why do you talk to yourself?" I've explained to them I am actually praying; I'm helping myself stay guarded in God's peace, so that the attacks that fly all around me will have no place to land!

What might this look like, you ask? I'm sure it looks as different as the various kinds of people who pray! But for me, here's how I approach it. In the morning, I offer specific prayers at a specific time. I carve out a time in the morning to meet with God, and I pray for the Lord to give me the strength to start my day. I ask that He would provide me anything specific I need to face my day, and I also ask that He'd help me be thankful for giving me another day to live for Him. Then, as the day unfolds, I pray in the moment for anything going on. I pray for wisdom to overcome various problems, and I thank Him for whatever is before me, because really, it is His faithfulness on display, giving me an opportunity for growth. (Sometimes it takes a second for me to remember this! Anybody else?) Before bed, I usually pray for my family and friends in need, or I lift up prayer requests I have gathered during the day, and I bring all these things to the Lord again to leave them in His hands. When I take the time to do this, I sleep with so much peace. Just knowing He is attentive to my cry, and that He's already working on every prayer, well, that just makes me feel flooded with His love and grace, and the anxiety lifts off of me. I can't explain it—maybe you know what I'm talking about if you've ever experienced this too—but I feel a wonderful element of mystery about such a divine peace that surpasses all understanding. What gifts we have in prayer and God's peace. It is freeing to know there is nothing I can do because I am a really busy mama, and I can't fix my own problems. I come to God for all my help in all those quick and crazy moments, and He hears me. More than that, He exchanges my anxieties for His strong and defensive peace that guards off worry and keeps me at rest in His presence.

How wonderful is our God to guard us this way in the middle of our chaos and our crazy?

PRAYER: Lord of Peace, I ask You for an abundance of Your guarding peace today. Through Your Spirit, I know You can produce this in me! My mind and heart are anxious—You know the worries I carry. And so I pray I'll find peace by trusting in You at all times. Help me stay in a prayer bubble with You all day long, so that I might be guarded by Your strong protection against any attacks. Help me learn to live in constant communication with You, just like You intended it to be from the beginning. I thank You that You're in control, that You hold my future, and that Your hands are strong to hold all my cares and concerns. I leave them with You right now, and I trust You to move on my behalf. In Jesus's name, Amen.

REFLECTION QUESTIONS

What mental image comes to mind when you think of peace? How does this verse square with that?

_____

_____

_____

_____

_____

_____

_____

_____

_____

_____

_____

_____

_____

_____

_____

_____

_____

_____

_____

_____

_____

_____

_____

_____

_____

_____

_____

_____

_____

_____

What usually brings on anxiety for you?

_____

_____

_____

_____

_____

What typically holds you back from bringing these worries, fears, troubles, or concerns to God?

_____

_____

_____

_____

_____

_____

_____

_____

_____

_____

_____

_____

_____

_____

_____

_____

_____

_____

_____

_____

_____

_____

_____

_____

How might you take a step toward more consistent prayer today?

_____

_____

_____

PEACE THAT STAYS TO THE END

PEACE // DAY 5

Now may the Lord of peace himself give
you peace at all times in every way. The Lord be with you all.

2 THESSALONIANS 3:16 (ESV)

"Goodness, look at this crazy world around us. Surely Jesus is coming back any moment!"

These words have probably been spoken by believers in every single generation since the early church! And the Christians reading Paul's words in the book of 2 Thessalonians are no different. In fact, some of them really did mistakenly believe Jesus had come back already! Paul spends the book of 2 Thessalonians helping to correct this thinking along with a few other issues going on in their community.

In his final prayer for them, Paul prays that the Lord would give them peace of mind that He was with them. Given that these believers were living in terror about the possibility of the "day of the Lord" being upon them, this reassurance was exactly what they needed to hear. Paul wanted them to know that, although they surely needed to focus on living holy lives in the meantime (while they waited for Jesus's return), they also had no reason to fear for their eternal future, as they had been reconciled with God by the blood of the cross. They didn't have to worry about those things if they were in Christ! In a world that feels like it is falling apart and at any moment Jesus could return, what peace this offers us! God has blessed us with His peace "at all times"—whether Jesus comes tomorrow or in a thousand years—and "in every way"—not just in ways we assume or expect.

This letter applies to us even now as we think about the coming of our Lord and imagine what life will look like on the other side of eternity. Like the Thessalonians, we should live in holiness, but we also should not fear one bit. We should enjoy the deep peace God provides for us—we are His, and we will be with Him forever in glory when He comes for us! Surely this is a peace that sees us through until the very end.

This is the kind of peace that stays. It has lasting power to get us through not just today, but every day after that until the very end. Have you experienced peace that is unshakable? The kind that does not let you be shaken in fear because you know where you are standing with God? I pray you do, friend. If you are in a true relationship with God, then that peace is available to you *right this very moment* through the Spirit who produces it in your heart! He testifies deep within you that you are a child of God, giving you confidence that when the "day of the Lord" appears—whenever that may come—you will be brought into His eternal family for good.

I have experienced this peace many times during 2020 and beyond. What a time that was! I'm sure you remember what life was like when a global pandemic spread across the world. That season is one that none of us will ever forget. All of the health issues, the losses, the politics consuming every news feed and social media post were overwhelming. But what I remember most is this: I had a peace I could not understand or explain. Even on days I was so tempted to worry about my own fate, the Spirit helped smother all that worry with God's peace, and all I could think of was God's plan.

I remember watching the news, and it didn't shake me like it had in the past. There was a season in early marriage where we didn't have cable. Not only could we not afford it at the time (we put every penny we had into growing our business and raising our first kid), but we also found it too distracting, worry-inducing, and anger-creating. Eventually we learned to keep up with what was going on through trustworthy sources of information whose goal was simply to report the facts (not get their viewers piping mad!). Even then, however, the news could get so overwhelming, tempting me to feel like the world was crashing down.

Here's the truth in all that: this isn't the first time in history people have felt like the world is falling apart. God is asking us to do the same things He trusted all those who came before us to do in their moments of confusion and fear: *trust Him even when it is difficult.* Even when the news says there's no point in trusting Him. Even when it looks like there's no hope. Those moments are the ones that change everything. I choose to trust in the Lord of peace to give me His comfort *at all times and in every way*. The Lord is with us—right here in this time. Even with this news. His peace was for those Thessalonians in their moments of terror, and it is for you and me, right now too. And it's powerful to help us through the worst of news, all the way through to the end. The Lord is with us until the end, and so is His peace. I believe that. Do you believe?

PRAYER: Heavenly Father, Lord of Peace, I thank You for the gift of prayer—the access it grants me to You! You know the terrors of my heart today, and the parts of our world that make me shrink back in fear or rise up in anger. You know the parts of the news, or the issues happening in the church, that cause me to question everything and worry about the future. You know the fears I carry about the final day of judgment that is coming for this world. Help me remember that just as Your peace was available to the Thessalonians in their moments of terror about "the day of the Lord," it is available to me too! Would You please grant me the peace I need at this time and supply me with Your everlasting peace "at all times and in every way"? Comfort me in Your presence, with the knowledge I am Your child and You will see me through. I thank You now for the ways You tend to my fears and I receive the blessing of Your presence and help. In Jesus's name, Amen.

REFLECTION QUESTIONS

What issues in our world today tend to make you most nervous, afraid, or angry?

What fears do you have about the day Jesus returns?

**What does the gospel promise
you, if you're a Christian,
about that day?**

**What does "holy living
in the meantime" communicate
about your beliefs in Christ's return?
What does living this way tell the world?**

REFLECTION AND REST

Use the last two days of this week to rest from reading, and instead, reflect on what you've learned. Use the journaling prompts and space below to process and enjoy what the Lord is doing in your heart.

1. What aspect of God's peace did you find most encouraging this week? Most surprising?

2. In what tangible ways do you see the fruit of peace being developed by God's Spirit in your heart and actions? Take some time to thank God for this fruitful work He's doing in you.

3. In this season of your life, which of these needs the most development in your heart? Circle one.

A Different Kind of Peace.   Peace that Guards.
Peace that Stays.   Peace with Others.

What are some practical next steps you can take to develop this?

_____

_____

_____

_____

_____

_____

_____

_____

_____

_____

FREESTYLE REFLECTION

Use this space below to pray, write out a meaningful passage of Scripture, or process anything God has placed on your heart this week.

GOD'S PATIENCE

PATIENCE // DAY 1

The Lord is not slow to fulfill his promise as some count
slowness, but is patient toward you, not wishing that any
should perish, but that all should reach repentance.

2 PETER 3:9 (ESV)

When it comes to some area of your life that is particularly challenging, or
perhaps some issue in society that is especially evil, are you ever tempted
to believe that God is taking too long to show up? Like He won't ever
show up to make things right? You aren't alone! Christians in the time of
2 Peter faced a similar struggle. They were tempted to forget that Jesus
really is coming back—that He'll show up in the end, coming to defeat
evil and purify the world, making way for a pristine, perfect, and new
heavens and earth. And so Peter encourages them to live as if this reality
is true—because it is! In the time line of eternity, it's just around the bend!

If you're anything like me, this raises a question. *If that's the case,
Peter, then why does it feel like it's taking forever for God to show up and
make the world right again?*

Today's verse gives us the answer. In the middle of stirring these
Christians up to live godly lives in view of eternity, he gives them some
comforting perspective on why eternity feels so far away. God isn't taking
forever, Peter says, nor is God neglectful of His children on this earth who
face all sorts of trials and tribulations. *He's being patient with the world*,
giving as much time as possible for repentance before He comes. God isn't
slow in fulfilling His promise to defeat evil and set things straight—He's
patient. Here we see that the perspective of heaven is so different than
the perspective of earth. In the end, the problem isn't God. The problem
is sin. The problem is the human heart. God does not hastily bring our
present moment in history to a quick end because He wishes for every

single one of those hearts to return to Him and find salvation before the coming judgment!

What kind of feelings do you experience when you hear what Peter is trying to say? Are you overcome with gratitude for the compassion and patience of our great Father toward everyone who does not yet know Him? I know I am! Where would I be if He had come before I came to know Him? Where would you be? Where would any of us be?

This verse in 2 Peter is just one example of the ways God Himself is patient. As you and I can probably both attest, He is patient in a million other ways. Do you have a story of God's patience in your life? I do. I remember giving my life to the Lord at the age of nine. I am so grateful for His gift of salvation, but I am sad to say that for a while I did nothing with it. I didn't open it to find out the deeper parts of what it meant or how it set me apart in this world. I was saved by the gospel, but I wasn't necessarily *walking* in it. I just continued with my life the only ways I knew how without a godly example.

Yet God's compassion for me continued to follow me even at such a tender age, and His patience with me was remarkable as I slowly grew up. He covered me with His protection and promises during the most challenging times of my life. He knew what I would go through in the future. He knew I would need Him. He knew how long it would take me to truly know Him at deeper levels. Whenever I prayed to Him on those nights I cried myself to sleep because my parents fought or my dad didn't come home, or my mom was sick, I knew He was there. I knew who to go to. Even though I wasn't aware of all the ways I should be walking out the gospel, I knew God was my only stability. I believe our souls understand who God is before we can even comprehend the deeper details about His character.

Many times, especially in the moments of hardship, I would pray and ask Him *why? Why do I even exist? Why all this suffering? What is my purpose?* He had the answer for me then, and He has it now. As I grew, God eventually revealed to me that the Bible had all the answers I needed and He had purposefully written it for me—for all of us. Even in my deepest moments of doubt and questioning, God was patient with me, and led me to the truth in doses I could handle.

As I grew and learned, God helped me along until I opened up the gift of my salvation at a deeper level when I turned eighteen. As I look back, I see He had so much patience with me as I stumbled forward. I may have known the basics, but as I grew and made my faith my own, He patiently directed my steps at every moment in the journey. I'll never forget the season I had a renewed resolve to follow Him. In childhood, we make certain decisions on our own, I believe I genuinely made a choice to give my life to Him in my early years. But most of our decisions aren't our own. In those teen years, I remember finally getting to make my own choices. I decided to graduate high school, get good grades, do my homework, and to run track and cross-country. Though I had previously lived in my parents' effects of poor decision making, I now had the chance to make my own decisions—better decisions. I had graduated, and I became a young adult. I started college, and apart from a small scholarship provided by two of my high school teachers (which would only cover about two semesters of eight total), it was clear I was totally on my own. I had no support. It took that place of desperation for me to see I had nobody but the Lord to help me, and that is when I decided to deeply dedicate my whole future to the Lord, and start growing more in my faith. It took desperation to reach dedication, and God's patience walked with me every step of the way from one to the other.

If God had come back during those years in between, I might've been scared. I'd probably assume I was not ready. That is where a lot of believers are right now, I imagine. And here is the encouragement: God is also patient with them. He waits for us all to experience true repentance, to dedicate ourselves fully to Him. We are all in different places on our path as we move forward in growth and faith. And all the while, *we* are the ones taking our sweet time, not God. He does not ask us to be patient with others in this life without going ahead of us and showing us what patience means. The whole reason the fruit of patience can flow out of our lives is because our God is the patient One, and He plants that seed in us, starting with our story. So what's yours? And how has God proven Himself patient in it?

PRAYER: Heavenly Father, thank You for the patience You have for everyone—not just for the unbeliever who needs a little more time to finally come to know You, but also for me! Thank You for Your compassion toward me and the patience You clearly display as You help me along in life. Thank You that You make it possible for me to seek You and indeed find You at each stage of my journey. I praise You for the protection You provide for me during the difficult times—the times You patiently wait for me to come to my senses and repent. You know the people in my life who have yet to trust You for life and salvation. Help them reach out to You honestly, so they might know You. Give them the strength to enjoy Your salvation, Your guiding help in the Word, and deep satisfaction in Your truth. Remind me that the only reason I can bear the fruit of patience in this life is because it's true of You first! In Jesus's name, Amen.

REFLECTION QUESTIONS

What situation in your life makes you feel like God is being slow, or taking forever to show up? Do you ever feel that way about Jesus coming back? Why or why not?

_____

_____

_____

_____

_____

_____

_____

_____

_____

_____

_____

_____

_____

_____

_____

_____

_____

Are you ready for Jesus's return? Do you desire Him to come quickly or do you desire His patience to last a little longer? Who in your life benefits from God's patient timetable of Jesus's return?

_____

_____

_____

_____

How have you seen God
be patient in your story?
List some examples.

Why do you think
it's important to remember
that the fruit of patience in our
life comes first from our God who
is patient? What happens when we
forget this?

WAITING ON GOD

PATIENCE // DAY 2

I waited patiently for the LORD;
he inclined to me and heard my cry.

PSALM 40:1 (ESV)

The art of waiting is almost nonexistent in our world today, am I right? I know I'm guilty of this! If we cannot get something delivered in under an hour (or heaven help us if it takes two days!) outside of our door, we will go hunt it down until we get it. Well . . . that is, if we have the energy or the time. Because going to hunt it down would take forever (and it would require us to stop at some red lights that take a whole sixty seconds before turning green)! If we are hungry, we can run to a drive-thru or pop something in the microwave. If we need groceries, we use that fast-shipping membership and get them pronto. If we want entertainment, we don't even have to buy a movie ticket anymore. We can just stream online *right now* with a few clicks of a button!

In a world like this, it makes sense that patience feels hard to come by. This is especially true when you are praying for a way out of a tough situation, a time of suffering, a specific trial, or a season of pain. Whatever the prayer request, we have a hard time when it seems like God isn't answering immediately, or when His answer is "not yet." We tend to think He's ignoring us, when really, the answer is just *waiting*. Have you been there? Goodness knows I have many times. I have one memory in particular—one of the longest waiting seasons I've ever experienced—that comes to mind.

There was a season in my teens that was very dark. I was hard at work in my studies, but I was also in a very dysfunctional and abusive relationship with a guy. I ended that relationship because (1) I knew the Lord was asking me to, and (2) I was no longer safe. I had endured physical and mental abuse, and my mother, concerned for my safety (and our financial situation), made a big decision to move back to the country I was born in, Mexico. I had been in America for almost seven years at this point, and I did not want to leave. This was a land that had brought so much help and safety and spiritual clarity for me. It was where I freshly dedicated my life to the Lord and learned to walk in the ways of Jesus! After seven years of learning and growing, going back to Mexico was the last thing I wanted to do. I did not want to return. I wanted to stay, pursue my education, and grow in the Lord without fear of those dark days behind me. But I had no choice. Though we tried and tried, my mom and I both had a very hard time finding jobs, and we didn't have money to pay next month's rent or for food. So, tearfully, we packed our things, got in the car, and started driving south.

I prayed to the Lord *so often* to make a way for me to stay. I prayed and I prayed. I beat down heaven's door. God is a way maker! Surely He'd intervene and help us! But it didn't happen. He didn't answer right away. My only option was to take my mom's best advice: "obedience." (My mother always told me that if only she had listened and obeyed her parents' wise instruction, nothing that she had gone through would have happened to her.) I took her advice, though I didn't understand it at the time, and left everything behind in the U.S.

It was tough, but it hadn't been the first time. I went in total obedience and trust—not ultimately in my mom, but in the Lord. He knew our situation. He heard my prayer, and clearly this was His will, somehow. That was the hardest decision I've ever had to make. The farther and farther we drove, the deeper and deeper the pain got.

I honestly did not know what I was going to do. I started working shortly after our arrival as a receptionist in a hotel. I worked a lot to keep myself distracted, and after that job, I started working a double job as a jewelry maker in a mall and babysitting for the owner of the jewelry store. I didn't know it at the time, but this was the year God had set apart for me to grow in my faith. I started going to church and reading my dusty Bible. I worked all week from Monday to Saturday, but Sundays were for the Lord. I took two buses and walked miles to get to church. I tried to join a Bible study, but I couldn't make it because of my job and transportation issues. So I joined an online Bible study. Every other night we would share what we read, and we shared our "golden nuggets" of truth the Lord gave us. When time for prayer requests rolled around, I always had the same prayer: *Lord, make a way for me to get back to the States and finish my studies.*

When I look back on that year of my life, all I remember is that I rotated a lot between praying and crying. I didn't know what to call it at the time, but I was doing what plenty of people in the Bible have had to do over and over again—*I was waiting on God.* This was the most patient I have ever been—or perhaps been forced to be. I was genuinely getting used to my new life, but at the same time, I was always at peace trusting God was working on my behalf. No matter what He chose to do with my situation, I knew He was to be trusted. That even though I wanted Him to bring me to a new place, *He* was the real prize.

Finally, one day, something miraculous happened. Though my mother had told me many times before that she'd "NEVER" let me go back, here she was in front of me, telling me I should! Come to find out, she had shared a conversation with her father, my grandpa, and somehow whatever he said convinced her to let me return to the States and finish my education since my visa was still active. If it weren't for this conversation my grandpa had with my mother—a conversation totally outside of my control!—I never would have returned to the U.S. While I was having conversations with God, He was orchestrating conversations around me that I had no idea about. Conversations that would change everything.

In the end, I had the funds to return and start my studies again because I had been doing extra jewelry on the side to save some money. The day came. The Lord opened a door for me to stay with a friend's family until I could get on my feet and rent a room. Here's the crazy part: *This whole process took exactly one year.* I had gotten in that car with my mom on a certain day of the month the year before, and on the *exact same day* of the month the next year, I came back. You just can't make this stuff up! Now that is what I call God's perfect timing.

"I waited patiently for the LORD; he inclined to me and heard my cry" (Ps. 40:1 ESV). This has proven true for me, even in the waiting. God didn't just hear my prayer and my cries, but He gave me *patience* to get through the dark times with perseverance. In granting me a season to strengthen my ability to wait on Him, I got to see His perfect timing unfold before my very eyes. (Did I mention He not only made a way but also months after my arrival, I met my now-husband? Had God not forced that hard season of patience upon me, or had I not chosen to obey, I never would have married him! This is another story for another day!)

Looking back on that story, I have to say that waiting on God was the hardest thing I have ever done, but it was also the best thing. Through the waiting, God helped me grow and heal. He gave me an extended season of refinement, where He was making me into a better version of myself. I was asking Him for one thing, but I can now see that the road He had me on would give me *more* than what I had originally asked for. God is worth waiting on! Friend, He hears you, and He'll equip you with patience while you wait. Let Him bear patience in you, even today, so that you'll look more like Him in the end. You won't regret it.

PRAYER: Oh, Father, thank You for hearing my prayers and my cries. Thank You for being so generous and patient toward me. I know I can trust Your ways and give You total control with my prayer requests—I know You'll work out everything for my good! If I have any problem laying down anything in Your presence, help me identify it and then release it, letting You work it out. I surrender it to You, even now! You know what I am waiting on in this season. I bring it to You in total trust that You are wise, that You know whether or not it needs to come to fruition—and if it does, You know the proper timing for that to happen far better than I do! Help me come to You over and over for patience—it is hard, but I know You can produce it in me! Help me trust in Your Word and Your plan for my life, even when I don't understand it. Help me wait on You well, because You are a God worth waiting for! In Jesus's name, Amen.

REFLECTION QUESTIONS

Do you have a season in your life when God taught you what patience looks like over the long haul? Record what that was like below.

What did you learn in the waiting process?

_____

_____

_____

_____

_____

_____

In what ways are you waiting on God in this current season of your life? While you wait to see how He'll handle this situation, how can you remind yourself *He* is the real prize?

_____

_____

_____

_____

_____

_____

_____

_____

_____

_____

_____

_____

_____

_____

_____

_____

_____

_____

Look back at your recorded memory above. How does that past season give you the strength you need to face this current season with patience?

_____

_____

_____

_____

_____

DON'T PLAY THE FOOL

PATIENCE // DAY 3

A patient person shows great understanding,
but a quick-tempered one promotes foolishness.

PROVERBS 14:29

If you are anything like me, you know you're not supposed to act foolishly in your life. You know better. You know you shouldn't let foolishness take over your life. After all, a fool's path only leads to destruction.

No one wants to be a fool. But have you ever wondered what creates foolishness? How is a fool made? What prods the wise person to leave the path of wisdom for the path of folly? There are a lot of answers to that question, but Proverbs 14:29 gives us one part of the answer. Foolishness happens, in part, because of impatience. When we are rash in our attempts to sort out a situation, or we are quick to become inflamed about something we don't like that isn't changing fast enough for us, we have surely stepped off the path of wisdom, onto the path of the fool.

Ouch! The Bible holds no punches here. Do you lack patience in a current situation? Are you quick-tempered when it is not shaking out the way you want it to? If so, God's Word is clear. This isn't a harmless character flaw or one of those "I'm only human" scenarios that all of us like to fall back on sometimes when we feel called out—this is promoting foolishness.

Lack of patience reveals a fool. This is quite convicting for me!

So what is the answer? How do we develop patience so that we don't play the fool? The Proverbs help us again here: "A person's insight gives him patience, and his virtue is to overlook an offense" (Prov. 19:11).

How does God develop the fruit of patience in us? By giving us insight. Most of the time when we face a circumstance we don't like, we get all hot and bothered because we can't see out of it. What we lack is insight and perspective into the situation; we lack a vantage point that could help us see the situation accurately. *Insight.* That's what guards us from being quick-tempered, impatient, rash, or foolish. Where might we find this insight and perspective? God's Word! It gives us the wisdom and the worldview we need to make sense of situations that would usually drive us mad.

For example, consider a family like mine during my growing-up years. Full of conflict and volatility. Maybe you know what that's like—that feeling that something will inevitably go wrong when you all get together. Whether it's your family or a certain group of friends (or maybe even online!), it can get so dark and difficult with that many conflictive people in one room. To this day, it is still hard for me to be in a room full of family members.

However, while it's difficult to be with them, it's much better than it used to be because now I have perspective going in—insight from God's Word. Where I might have once gone in with a quick temper and lack of patience, now I have a higher perspective on what's really going on. First, I know the division and fighting in my family is not "life as usual." Because I know the story of the Bible, I know my family was not supposed to be that way. God wants something better. He created a better world in the beginning, and He's in the process of restoring it. And I also know sin is to blame for hurtful things that go on in families like mine. I also know, because of God's Word, there's an enemy who is always lurking and ready to attack each person in the room in specific ways, depending on their weaknesses. Now, I try to be mentally prepared to keep my patience on guard against any sin in my own heart and against any attack by the enemy when I enter the presence of my family. After all, the enemy really knows how to hinder you by using people you love the most to hurt you, where it hurts the most. On top of these things, God's Word has taught me that every person on the planet has an idol they love more than God, and when an idol is threatened, people get *mad.*

Because of all these lessons the Bible has taught me, I see my family's situation differently than I did before. Their angry outbursts and foolish actions are not just random. Yes, those things may impact me deeply, but at the bottom of things, they aren't even about me. Those issues in my family are either due to their own sin, suffering, idol-worship, or struggle against the enemy! They are freaking out (and taking their issues out on the wrong people) because they don't have insight. Just like I once couldn't, they can't see out of their circumstances or feelings. They are trapped inside with no higher perspective.

Do you see how insight gives us patience? Even compassion? None of this means that the wounds from my family don't hurt or I don't get sad about the various situations they are in—I do. But ultimately it means I'm able to bear with all those things in patience instead of anger, because the Word of God has prepared me with wisdom and insight into the situation. I don't have to be rash. I know what's going on, and I can patiently walk through it because Scripture has given me eyes to see from a different vantage point.

This is how wisdom and patience keep anger under control. This process allows us to have patience always on guard against anything that comes our way. So, friend, guard yourself with the kind of patience that comes from insight. It will get you through the most maddening situations. Let the Lord's patience fuel you, and let it kick in, especially in the moments you want to retaliate with harsh words. Know that it's God's job to develop them in the areas they are out of line. He has the power to point out their sin and work in them as He has done in you and me. Remember the Scripture's perspective: the real reason why people hurt others is because they are hurting and there is pain inside them—pain that comes from the Fall, from sin, from suffering, and from the enemy.

Those hard moments in your history, in your family, or in that circle of friends—they don't define you, but they can make you stronger in patience. They can give you opportunities to stay on the path of wisdom, even when you feel the pull to step on the path of the fool. It may not be family for you, but whatever it is, know this: God will use any pain and difficulty to refine your character and make you more patient, like Him.

PRAYER: Heavenly Father, thank You for the fruit of patience You are developing in me through Your Spirit. Your insight is what I need in the most difficult times, for it will help me endure the challenges and the trials, being patient instead of angry. Please help me control my anger before it takes over me. Remind me what's true in Your Word, and help me see the world—and my trials—through its lens. I know I am a walking representative of You. Help me grow in patience so I might reflect Your character more and more—not just for others, but for Your glory. I surrender now any anger, pain, or pride so that none of these things will hinder the fruitfulness You are cultivating in me. In the name of Jesus, Amen.

REFLECTION QUESTIONS

If you had to explain the path of wisdom versus the path of the fool to a friend, how would you describe the two paths in your own words?

Is there something that God is specifically convicting you about in regard to patience? What is it?

If a weakness, what did today's devotional teach you that you might need to pursue in order to experience more patience?

PATIENCE WITH OTHERS

PATIENCE // DAY 4

And we urge you, brothers, admonish the idle, encourage the fainthearted, help the weak, be patient with them all.

1 THESSALONIANS 5:14 (ESV)

Have you ever led a group of people who seemed more like a circus than willing participants? Maybe you led a group project as a student many years ago, and you had an interesting cast of project members. Or maybe you've led a small group at your church, and your group was chock-full of . . . how shall we say this . . . *personality*. Maybe you are reading this right now and thinking, *Friend, what you're describing is basically just parenting children!* Regardless of the specifics, we all know what it's like to "herd cats."

No matter the type of group, the members have all sorts of reasons why they resist being led in a certain direction. Some won't go in the right direction simply because they are lazy. Others won't keep up because they are fearful and don't think they can do it. Others mean well, but they are weak, and they need assistance or extra strength to help them to make it across the finish line. Some are just plain proud and stubborn, and refuse to move unless the direction is their idea.

Here's some encouragement for you: the leaders in the church of Thessalonica totally get it. In fact, they get it so much that Paul wrote them a letter to help them deal with problems just like this.

Some church members were lazy—they were taking advantage of others so they wouldn't have to work. Others were terrified by the threat of persecution and deaths, which were happening around them so quickly. Others were weak in spiritual maturity, while still others were weak physically. The list could go on.

What was Paul's advice to the leader? *Run for it! Because these people are never going to get it and you just need to move on!* That might be what you and I would advise after a long season of herding cats. But no. Thankfully, that's not what Paul said. Paul told them to meet the church members where they were and give them exactly what they needed. He told them to warn the lazy people, comfort the fearful, and uphold the weak. And above everything? *Be patient with them all.*

That sounds like a high calling, and it is. But here's the encouraging part: the leaders weren't asked to do anything the Lord hadn't done already for all of us! Think about it: all of those things and more have been given to us through Christ. The Lord has warned us against sin and where sin can drag us. More than that, He paid for all that sin! He is also our comforter so we can find peace in any circumstance. He also upholds us and gives us strength when we seem to have none. He has been patient with all of us as we grow, slowly but surely. He pushes us out of our comfort zone when we get stubborn. While these leaders could never be Jesus Himself, Paul is helping them follow in Jesus's footsteps, shepherding His flock with the care and patience produced in their hearts by His Spirit.

If you're a leader of others in some sort of group, perhaps you need to hear that Jesus really can give you the patience you need to lead the members. Perhaps God is calling you to warn, encourage, admonish, uphold, comfort, and help them in specific ways, depending on the struggle of each person. And, more than that, perhaps He's asking you to keep doing these things on repeat, which requires a lot of patience. People don't change or move easily! Just remember, friend, He is not asking you to do something for them that He hasn't already done for you. Remember to enjoy the ways He does all these things for you, so that you can minister as His instrument, His love for them flowing through you. Receive these things for yourself from Jesus before you try to pour them out on others! Take inventory on how He's been ever-patient with you, so that you might have the patience to keep ministering to them in His name.

If you happen to be a participant in a group, try to identify what kind of "sheep" you are in the mix. If a stranger happened upon the group, how would they probably identify you? The one who struggles with idleness? The one who struggles with fear? With weakness? With pride? Now, for a moment, shift your gaze over to the leader. How has God been patient with you through him or her? How has this person, over time, shown you patience in your specific struggles?

I can recall many situations where, as a follower in a group, I was slow-moving in an area I really needed to grow in. The most important and life-changing one was concerning my spiritual growth. I remember a season when I called myself a follower of Christ, but I was lazy toward reading and studying His Word. I only attended Sunday services, as if checking that box off would make me holy. In short, I lived a life of spiritual starvation from Sunday to Sunday. I mean, imagine if you only ate once a week. That was me, trying to make one Sunday "meal" last all week long. I was too weak, run down, and lazy to move toward the knowledge of the Lord. There He was, available to me day and night, a table full of the Bread of Life and Living Water and fruitfulness. But I just walked around it in starvation by my own choice!

God knew this was a weak spot for me. And I'm sure my leaders noticed too. One fateful day, my pastor spoke about spiritual growth. He posed a question: *How are we supposed to grow without opening His Living Word, and being nourished by it?* I realized that being a Christian was not a magic trick. I had to apply some effort to look for sin in my life, learn His Word, be filled by His wisdom, and change—not because I had to but because I wanted to.

Thank God my pastor kept leading us in that season. Thank God he kept "warning the idle" and "helping the weak," because I was one of them who needed such a leader! I'm so grateful for the message that rebuked me and instructed me toward God's nourishing Word and His everlasting ways.

Whether you're a leader or a participant, God wants us to know we are not enemies (2 Thess. 3:15). We are family, and we should treat one another as children of the most powerful Father. Though we have different struggles and different spiritual growth rates, in the end, we are not any different than the person next to us. God knows we all need to be developed in various ways, which is why He instructs us to help one another, build one another up, and encourage one another always. Building one another up might look like warning one person, while it looks like upholding or comforting or rebuking or helping another. It may look like encouraging someone with His Word or reminding someone of His promises. It may look like doing something when you see someone down, instead of waiting until someone else helps. It may look like stopping, even if you are busy, to pray with someone. It may look like "accept[ing] the one who is weak in the faith," or maybe even new and immature, "without passing judgment on his opinions" (Rom. 14:1 NASB1995), because after all, we all start *somewhere* in our faith journey! It may look like a million different things, but all of it looks like patience. We are to be patient with everyone, not because it's easy or natural, but because we've been given the same kind of patience and long-suffering from God, who has uplifted us in our stubborn and weak seasons alike. So who are we not to turn around and do the same?

Don't lose heart, friend. Whether you are the giving end of patience or the receiving end, God is able to provide it abundantly in your relationships. Choose to obey His instruction, and watch Him work!

PRAYER: Lord, thank You for extending so much grace, patience, and love to me! I ask for patience with my brothers and sisters in Christ. You know the ones in my group or circle—the ones who are hard to be patient with. Help me remember no matter where each of us is in our spiritual journey, You've made it possible for us to grow together and build one another up. I pray You help me guide others with the example that You have given me. I pray You'll inspect my heart, and reveal to me where I resist loving others. Give me the strength to better serve them in the patience You provide. Help me see exactly what they need to move forward in their faith—a warning, an encouragement, some help, or a hand to uphold and comfort them. Help me remember that You do these very same things for me every single day in Your great patience! In Jesus's name, Amen.

REFLECTION QUESTIONS

In this season of life, do you play the role of a leader or a participant? How so?

What has been your biggest struggle in this role?

Who in your life do you resist leading with patience? Why?

_____

_____

_____

_____

_____

_____

_____

_____

_____

_____

_____

_____

_____

_____

_____

_____

_____

_____

_____

_____

_____

_____

_____

_____

How has today's verse specifically spoken to that resistance you feel? Did anything in particular jump out at you from the verse?

PATIENCE IN DIFFICULTY

PATIENCE // DAY 5

Rejoice in hope; be patient in affliction; be persistent in prayer.

ROMANS 12:12

I can't remember where I heard this story, but here's how it goes. There was once a man who came into a massive inheritance—as in *billions* of dollars. He received a phone call from an attorney, telling him he had a rich uncle who had died, leaving him a fortune. The only thing the man had to do was get to the bank to officially receive the funds in person. On the way to the bank, his car broke down and popped a tire too. There was no way he was getting to the bank in that car! After taking a moment to restabilize and gather himself, the man considered his options. And you know what he did? He left the car right where it was, on the side of the interstate, totally unphased by losing it, and skipped the rest of the way to the bank on foot!

If you are anything like me, you wouldn't be *skipping* anywhere if your car broke down and popped a flat tire—especially not on an interstate. You'd probably be throwing your hands up and wondering *Why, God, why?!*

So why in the world did that man consider his car trouble no big deal? The answer is easy: because compared to the billions of dollars he was about to inherit, the car was a drop in the bucket. Getting upset about the car would be like getting sidetracked over a few pennies while staring at a ten-million-dollar bill.

Difficulty, for the Christian, is like the car. It's just a bump in the road on the way toward our eternal inheritance in Christ. Those bumps are real—they destabilize us for a moment, or shake us a bit as we try to navigate around them. Feeling poked and prodded by the sharp edges of this life is normal. And we should run to God in those difficult and dark moments. But they have no right to take our hope for the future. Nor do they have the right to take our patience as we wait for our glorious eternal fate to come. Patience isn't nearly as hard to maintain for the Christian when we know what's ahead.

You know what else the car did? It tested if the man believed in his inheritance. It forced him to consider which thing to give the majority of his time, attention, energy, and affection toward, and to run hard after the most important thing. Where he might've been impatient and angry with his car trouble before, he was now able to be patient through it—eager and rejoicing even—because he knew what was coming for him! As Romans 8:25 says, "Now if we hope for what we do not see, we eagerly wait for it with patience."

Without difficulties, our faith in God's promises cannot be tested or refined. If the trials never come, we're never forced to consider which "thing" we're living for, and whether or not we think the trek to our eternal inheritance is worth it. As hard as challenges of this life are, not having them might be worse, for then we'd never experience the very things that create not only patience in us, but a stronger faith—a *proven* faith. We might assume our faith in and our patience for our eternal future is real, but without the testing that comes with difficulties, we'd never know for sure.

Do you trust that you will one day see His glory and that some day in the not-so-distant future, you'll finally be able to see the way His perfect plan worked together for good in your life, even through the dark and difficult times? Because you will! He promises you that!

I like to think God gives us little previews of that coming day when all will be made clear. There are times, even on our side of eternity, when He gives us moments of clear spiritual hindsight. It's like we can finally see, even if it's just a glimpse, what He was doing in some past season—a season we did not understand in the moment. Have you ever gone through something like that? Something you did not understand at the time, but years later, God revealed to you what He was up to? Have you ever looked back and thought, *Wow, God knew what He was doing. Somehow, it worked out in the end. I should have just trusted Him all those years ago and been patient through the process. He had a good plan all along!* If God can reveal things like this to us in various moments of our story on this side of heaven, imagine what we'll be saying to ourselves about our whole lives once heaven actually comes to earth! We'll be wishing we could stare ourselves in the face right this minute, grab ourselves by the shoulders and say, *Patience, my dear. He knew what He was doing. Even in this. You'll see. It will make sense. He is up to something glorious right now. I know it's hard. But don't try to be a little god yourself and solve this one on your own. Have patience.*

As always, when it comes to where we should look to learn about patience in difficulty, we must look to Christ. We must let the King of kings guide us. Over and over as we look at Jesus in Scripture, we see Him being patient with trials and tribulations. At the start of His ministry, we see His patience on display as He fasts from food and resists the devil. During His ministry, we see His constant patience in action as He kindly guides His stubborn disciples and faces rejection from His own hometown. And at the end of His earthly ministry, we clearly see His long-suffering on our behalf, even in death!

As we follow Christ's example, we must be prepared not to only observe patience in His life, but also exercise it in our own. It doesn't come naturally, but it can be developed through the Spirit's power and our participation! Exercising patience is a lot like exercising our physical bodies. For me, after having three children, it has been a challenge to get back into a steady rhythm of working out. Every time I go to a weight training day at the gym with my husband, I warn him about the next day. *Babe, get ready—I'm gonna be so sore tomorrow; I'll need your help to get up from the bed or the couch!* My husband likes to remind me that "soreness is weakness leaving the body." Believe me, after weight training, I am more aware of my weakest muscles, and I know where I need the most work. The same is true with the pain we experience through difficulties. When we entrust the pain to God and remain steadfast, that is weakness leaving our spiritual lives, being replaced with patience!

Ultimately the difficulties and challenges of our life force us to lean in to God and learn more about the God who is patient with us. Take heart, friend, and stay focused. Whatever the storm is for you, you'll find that on the other side of it, you are more long-suffering and patient than you were before—more like your God!

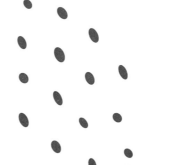

PRAYER: Lord Jesus, You know the storm I face today! I tend to think You aren't at work in the midst of it sometimes, but I know one day I'll look back and see what You were up to! Give me the patience in the meantime, I pray. Help me endure, and fill me with Your joy and peace. Remind me of all Your beautiful promises as I wait out this storm, and help me entrust the pain to You. Thank You for Your perfect example of patience in Scripture. In it, I see the guidance I need to walk through adversity in a godly way. Keep me close to You, and help me trust in Your perfect timing for the tough situation I find myself in. When this storm passes, I want to give You the glory for the victory. Help me remember that endurance is possible with You by my side, and my future inheritance eclipses any temporary affliction I face today. In the Holy name of Jesus we pray, Amen!

REFLECTION QUESTIONS

Looking back over your life, can you think of a tough situation where you thought God was absent, only to find out later that He was there after all, and He had worked it all out? Record this memory in the space provided.

What difficulties or adversity do you face today? What storm are you walking through?

_____

_____

_____

Practically speaking, what would exercising patience look like for you in this storm?

_____

_____

_____

_____

_____

_____

_____

_____

_____

_____

_____

_____

_____

_____

_____

_____

_____

_____

_____

Explain below how your temporary difficulties compare to the future inheritance you have in Christ.

_____

_____

_____

_____

REFLECTION AND REST

Use the last two days of this week to rest from reading, and instead, reflect on what you've learned. Use the journaling prompts and space below to process and enjoy what the Lord is doing in your heart.

1. What aspect of God's patience did you find most encouraging this week? Most surprising?

_____

_____

_____

_____

_____

_____

_____

2. In what tangible ways do you see the fruit of patience being developed by God's Spirit in your heart and actions? Take some time to thank God for this fruitful work He's doing in you.

_____

_____

_____

_____

_____

_____

_____

_____

3. In this season of your life, which of these needs the most development in your heart? Circle one.

**Waiting on God.   Not Playing the Fool.
Patience with Others.   Patience in Difficulty.**

What are some practical next steps you can take to develop this?

_____

_____

_____

_____

_____

_____

_____

_____

_____

_____

_____

_____

_____

FREESTYLE REFLECTION

Use this space below to pray, write out a meaningful passage of Scripture, or process anything God has placed on your heart this week.

GOD'S KINDNESS

KINDNESS // DAY 1

God can point to us in all future ages as examples of the incredible wealth of his grace and kindness toward us, as shown in all he has done for us who are united with Christ Jesus.

EPHESIANS 2:7 (NLT)

Is there a time in your life, or perhaps a certain situation, when you're tempted to say, "No way, no how, was God proving Himself kind here. How in the world could God be kind in *that* kind of circumstance?"

If anyone should have the right to doubt God's kindness in this way, it's the apostle Paul—*especially* while writing the book of Ephesians. He's in a prison cell as he writes! Locked in chains! Why? For simply being a faithful witness to Jesus in a world that didn't want to hear about it.

Of anything he could write in that moment, what words does he scratch down as he waits in his cell? Of all the things that could be on his mind, what consumes his thoughts in this terrible moment? The incredible wealth of God's grace and kindness! Paul was grateful for God's kindness—for what the Lord had redeemed him from. God knew his sin—that in his past he had persecuted Christians. And still, God revealed Himself to Paul and saved him. Though he was once bound by sin, now he was liberated by the gospel of Christ Jesus!

While there are plenty of ways God shows Himself kind in this life (His care for the world, His sustaining power to bring forth the seasons, His provision for our meals, His generosity in giving us relationships with people we love dearly), the truest name and fullest definition of God's kindness is Christ Jesus. God gave us the most intimate and rich gift in His Son. If you're a parent, imagine giving your kid up for a bunch of terrible sinners who spit on your name and raise their fist against you—no way! Not my babies! Sorry, humanity! Thank God I am not God. Because if I were, you, dear friend and reader, would probably not be saved!

One of the best parts of God's kindness is that—like every other fruit of His Spirit—it flows out of Him, into His people, and back out again to everyone around them. I know that's been true for certain believers in my life. Every time I think about them, I am overwhelmed. Through them, God's kindness attracted me to the faith. For example, the family member who introduced me to Jesus Christ was so kind that I thought she was fake. But you know what? I wanted what she had. Even though I didn't understand why she would look out for us and care for a family she never had contact with before, I knew I wanted to be like her somehow. Or think of Paul! When he sat in a prison cell, God's kindness flowed through him to his jailer! Do you remember the story in Acts 16? Though he was miraculously freed from his prison, he chose to stay. Why? Because the jailer would lose his life if he lost one of his prisoners. In fear of losing Paul now that the prison doors were open, the jailer tried to kill himself. To keep the jailer from taking his own life, Paul stayed put in that prison cell instead of making a run for it, and he offered his jailer the gospel. Paul knew to be kind to others because he had richly received God's kindness for himself. Think of that—Paul spent his time in jail cells writing letters to the early churches of the time, spreading kindness to his jail mates, and saving the life of his oppressors!

You just can't fake that sort of love for other people. No matter who you are, *only experiencing God's kindness for yourself can make you that sort of person.*

Are you kind? I know for a lot of us, it doesn't come naturally. But why not? In Colossians 3:12 (ESV), we are told to "put on then, as God's chosen ones, holy and beloved, compassionate hearts, kindness, humility, meekness, and patience." The Bible wouldn't call us to this if it weren't possible, so why do we resist? Given how kind God has been to us, and given that His Spirit grows this fruit in us over time, we have no excuse not to be kind to one another. The answer behind why we aren't kind sometimes is what the Bible calls "the flesh." Our flesh is at war with the Spirit inside us, and it tries to get us to choose selfishness over sacrificial kindness. But we have the power to resist that. We really do have the power to be kind. Even if we face someone rude, unloving, or hurtful, we can take it as a God-given opportunity to show His kindness. We can interpret it as our own personal "prison jailer" sent from the Lord to us—a "jailer" who does not have eyes to see the sin they are committing and desperately needs to see the gospel on display in our response to them!

What I love about kindness is that nobody can fight and win over it. Kindness always conquers and changes attitudes. Did you know that's true not just for us, but for God? Romans 2:4 says it is God's *kindness* that leads people to repentance and change! Not His wrath or His anger or His quick comebacks or His threats. His *kindness*. We could not fight it or win over it. It conquered us and changed us! (More on that tomorrow!)

Even when we fail, God still chooses to show His riches in kindness toward us. No matter what our "prison cell" is today, let's take some time to revel in the "incredible wealth" we have in such a kind God!

PRAYER: Oh Lord, Your kindness brings me to my knees and reminds me of all the ways You've been lavishly generous with me from the beginning. I feel so thankful and honored as I realized You have kindly protected me from more than I will ever know. And even in the hard places You chose not to deliver me from, Your kindness was still there by my side, sustaining me and using me as a vessel for good! Help me remember Your ultimate act of kindness—giving me Christ, Your Son, who freed me from sin and death! Please, Lord, bear more fruit of kindness in my heart today. Teach me to be like You. Give me Your heart and kindness for others, and let it flow out of me so others might better know Your character. In Jesus's name, Amen!

REFLECTION QUESTIONS

How has God been unfathomably kind to you? Record some instances here.

When are you most tempted to believe God is not kind?

How does Paul's story encourage you in that temptation?

_____

_____

_____

_____

_____

_____

_____

_____

_____

_____

_____

_____

_____

_____

_____

_____

_____

_____

_____

_____

_____

_____

_____

_____

Why is true kindness impossible without the Spirit's work in your heart?

_____

_____

_____

A KINDNESS THAT CHANGES US

KINDNESS // DAY 2

Or do you despise the riches of his kindness, restraint, and patience, not recognizing that God's kindness is intended to lead you to repentance?

ROMANS 2:4

As believers, we might think that we understand the scale and meaning of God's kindness, but we really don't. We simply cannot fathom it!

What do you think God's kindness is, exactly? Is it just a nice, vague sense of warmheartedness from heaven? Is it God's good intentions or "good vibes" toward us, from afar? Or is it stronger than that? Is it just a feeling? Or does it *do* something in some way? When the kindness approaches us, how does it act?

Good thing God has spoken on the matter!

Look at Titus 3:4–5a: "But when the *kindness* of God our Savior and his love for mankind appeared, *he saved us*—not by works of righteousness that we had done, but according to his mercy."

When God's kindness appears, we see that it doesn't just radiate good feelings. It *does* something. When God's kindness comes on the scene, it *saves*. It did this in our conversion to Christ, as this verse points to, and it also does this every day after that. Our God's riches keep on giving before and after the fact! Friend, God's kindness doesn't just want to give you warm fuzzies to make you feel better; it wants to *rescue* you, no matter what you face!

You know what else God's kindness does to us? It *changes* us. Re-read our verse for today up above, and soak it in. God's kindness is the thing that leads us to repentance, which is just a fancy word for *change*. As believers, we always want to be transforming, don't we? We want to keep growing so we can look more and more like Jesus over time.

And what helps us do that? God's kindness! The more we experience His kindness, the more we change! It is surprising this verse does not say "God's wrath" or "God's judgment" or "God's holiness" leads us to repentance. All those things are true about God, and they certainly make us stand in awe. But of all the things the Bible could say changes a person to the point of repentance, it is God's tender, rescuing kindness that brings us to our knees, drops our jaws, and makes us turn around, away from sin and toward righteousness. He always has a plan to work in us and to help us grow—who would have thought that His kindness is a primary way He works this out?

Knowing these things about God's kindness changes everything when it comes to approaching Him in prayer, am I right? I mean, what do your honest prayers begin with? Now that I know the truth about God's kindness, my honest prayers always start with "HELP!" I can come to God in this sort of vulnerability, unafraid, because I know His kindness wants to rescue me and change me!

Most of the time, it is really hard to admit my wrongs in front of others, but not in front of God! His kindness is ready to help! And when it meets me, it brings me to my knees and produces repentance. His kindness changes my heart! Friend, don't be afraid to admit your wrongs, failures, and your weakness. God's response toward you is tender and He's ready to aid you. And He is magnified when we humble ourselves, reaching out for His kindness.

I know this to be true when I think of the plan I once had for my life. I told the Lord, "God, I am not going to get married or have children. I will just live and serve You." My reason for not getting married was because my parents' marriage was really scary, and it inflicted too much pain on me. I thought every husband and wife would be like my mom and dad. I thought every family would be like mine, and that if kids were ever in the picture, they'd end up suffering the same way I did. I thought avoiding a family altogether would make me happy. Never did I read or listen to the Lord on such an important topic. The Bible has a lot to say about loneliness, family, and marriage, but I didn't want to even ask God for His opinion because I thought I knew it all better.

Fast-forward to the season when I got to return to the States and to my studies. It was really hard finding work, but I was finally able to get a job working on campus for a coach. I needed that job so bad! I cleaned my coach's office, helped him with his emails, and did other office work he would somehow create for me to do. Looking back, I now see this coach was really the father I always wished I had! He knew how much I needed the work, and apart from just providing that, he would also guide me through how to make the best decisions, and he always helped me to stay safe. Little did I know, he wanted me to meet someone he had in mind. I told him a relationship was not something I was looking for. So, organically over time, he eventually introduced me to my now husband in a very kind, unassuming, and nonthreatening way.

Never had I met a guy like my future husband! I was sure it was too good to be true, so I tested him in small ways. Part of me wanted him to not like me just so I could prove myself right—all men were like my dad! But somehow, he passed every test and proved to be a stand-up guy. I would ask people, *is he real?* I just couldn't believe how God-fearing he was, how respectful, and how kind. I called out to the Lord for help. I needed Him to rescue me from my deep fear, to change my heart, if I was ever going to brave something like marriage. And you know what? He did! He rescued me from the fear and He changed me. It was after a while of so much kindness coming at me that my whole demeanor changed. I stopped resisting what God had planned for me and I repented, turning away from the path I thought I wanted, toward the path the Lord was leading me toward. Where I was once all "no way, Lord—take him away!" I was now obedient, moving past the fear, and excited to move forward in marriage. *Kindness* was the game-changer.

In the end, God's kindness added to my life so much more than what I wanted or thought was possible. And you know what? His abundant kindness kept multiplying then, and it has not stopped after ten years of marriage and now three children!

It may not be marriage for you, but has something like this happened to you? Have you resisted God in some way, only to be totally changed later, because of His kindness and His readiness to help you? Friend, let's allow God's kindness to break in and save us, no matter where we are in the journey. Let's let it wash over our souls today, and move us to repentance and change!

PRAYER: Oh Lord, thank You for the kind of heavenly kindness that brings me to a state of clarity and repentance! There are so many things I presume as good for myself, but You have so many other good things for me—things I can't even fathom—if I'd only trust You as able to rescue me and change me! You know the ways I am resisting in You today. I call out for help and ask You to save me from my fear or anxiety about it, and transform me over time. Ultimately, I thank You for the kindness of the cross, which brought me to turn to You in my conversion. On the days I forget You love me and You're kind to me, help me remember the lengths You went to so that I might be saved! In Jesus's name, Amen.

REFLECTION QUESTIONS

What things usually tempts you to believe God is not kind to you?

How does the cross speak to these things?

_____

Why do you sometimes avoid approaching God for help? (Do you assume, perhaps, that His posture toward you is something other than kind? If so, what posture do you mistakenly assume He takes?)

_____
_____
_____
_____

_____
_____
_____
_____
_____
_____
_____
_____
_____
_____
_____
_____
_____
_____
_____
_____
_____
_____
_____

Looking back on key situations in your life, when were you changed by God's kindness to you? How does that help you trust Him with tough situations you face today?

_____
_____
_____
_____

KIND IN COMPASSION AND COMFORT

KINDNESS // DAY 3

Blessed be the God and Father of our Lord Jesus Christ, the Father of mercies and God of all comfort, who comforts us in all our affliction, so that we may be able to comfort those who are in any affliction, with the comfort with which we ourselves are comforted by God.

2 CORINTHIANS 1:3–4 (ESV)

What does the Son of God, Jesus Christ, our Lord and Savior, grant us when it comes to His Father? Most of us would say because of Christ's holy blood shed at the cross, we are granted *forgiveness* before the Father. And that is true! We'd also might say that Jesus's sacrifice on the cross grants us *access* to the Father, or maybe *right standing* before the Father. And those things are true too!

But of all the blessings the gospel brings to us, we often forget one—the comfort of God the Father. Because Jesus reconciled us to the Father, we now get to enjoy His tender, fatherly care and concern over us, no matter what challenges we face. The work of Christ didn't just bring you to God, friend, and then leave you at the door. The work of Christ brings you into the house, into the living room, and onto the lap of your Divine Dad, where you can bask in His kindness and compassion over you in your worst moments of affliction and pain. Where you were once distant and estranged from God, now your Father can comfort you as He extends His loving-kindness toward you. Isn't that the best news? We now have a forever-father who made a way for us to find refuge and safety in His comfort every single day! When was the last time you pointed to *that* as a blessing of the cross? I know I forget this far too often!

The apostle Paul, wrote our verse for today. He penned these words in a very personal letter to the church in Corinth. And all this talk of affliction isn't hypothetical—Paul *knows* affliction because he's been through it! He is explaining to them that in his weakness and in affliction, God comes close and makes Himself known. He calls God the "Father of mercies" and the "God of all comfort" for a reason: because he's experienced God's tender kindness to him in the darkest moments life could throw at him.

Next, Paul goes on to reveal the reason God comforts us—not only because He loves us, but because He knows when we experience His comfort, it changes us, and makes us more comforting and compassionate toward others. Did you catch that? As God comforts us and fills us with His kindness, that tenderness flows through us, moving outward, so we might comfort others with the same care we were given! Believers are called to comfort one another in our weakness and afflictions because we follow a God who does this for us. In His care for us, He develops us into compassionate people.

Do you view your hardships that way? As an opportunity to receive God's comfort, so that you might be a better conduit of that comfort for others? Heaven knows it can be hard to have this perspective when you are going through a rough patch! But what if we shifted our mindset and started to view our afflictions this way? What if we had *others* on our mind as we walked through the valley, seeing this stretch of the journey as the training ground to become more compassionate toward those who struggle similarly?

Just think of it. There might be a future situation where you are the only one around to help someone in a similar situation who really needs the help. There might be a time coming, just around the bend, when you are the chosen instrument to transfer the Father's encouragement and comfort straight into the heart of a struggler. There might be a circumstance where you are the only person who can relate to a certain struggler in a divinely orchestrated moment. And *you'll be ready* to answer the call to help them, all because God decided to develop you in your current moment of affliction! Whatever affliction you face right now—whatever shape it takes or move it makes—remember that it might be in your life so that you can not only learn what divine comfort feels like, but *pass it on* to a fellow struggler instead of avoiding them! In this way, your afflictions do not get the final word! God's Spirit uses these dark moments in your story to develop you into a person who can see like Him, act like Him, and *love* like Him as you walk forward in the world with those who have dark moments in their stories, too. The enemy might seek to make you afflicted in this life, but only God's Spirit can take that and make you kind!

Are you a comforter? I've had times when the answer has been yes and the answer has been no. And you know what I have learned? That I am not doing what God has called me to do if I am in my comfort zone. Isn't that something? *Comforters don't stay in their comfort zone! Jesus surely didn't.* In order to come close and comfort us, He had to leave His heavenly dwelling and get uncomfortable!

If I am about to do something that feels super-comfortable to me, I've learned I need to stop and pray about it, because very often it is not from the Lord. On the other hand, when I challenge myself to really put compassion and comfort on display, it's pretty inconvenient! For example, when I feel called to go drop coffee on someone's doorstep, it always seems to happen when I look early-morning-crazy. But I have to choose others and forget about my ego, risking the chance that someone sees me in my disheveled state. Or, for example, if I hear someone crying, I have to risk looking *for-real* crazy as I stop and reach out to them, trying to listen to them, even though they don't know me. As I walk away after the fact, I have to put off thoughts of fear or shame, not worrying about what they thought about me. Maybe they thought I was insane, or maybe they felt loved and cared for. In the end, their view of me doesn't matter. The real victory is that I did what God set out for me to do. The real win is that I saw an opportunity and I took it, because who knows if that person will hear the gospel again? Who knows if they'll ever have a chance to know that their Father longs to be reconciled to them, and wants to comfort them?

If you are enduring affliction, friend, run to the God of comfort. The Father of mercies stands ready to pour out His kindness and compassion over you. And once you are full of all that care and tenderness from His heart, let it overflow on someone else! Or, as I like to say, *go out of your way to encourage someone today.* They need it. We all do!

PRAYER: Heavenly Father, thank You for every good thing You have given me through Your Son Jesus, including the blessing of Your comfort! And thank You for making something good out of my hardships! Please help shift my perspective. Please help me see my current afflictions as opportunities to be filled up by Your kindness and comforted by Your fatherly care. More than that, help me see the rough patches in my life as chances to be developed into a kind, compassionate follower of You. I pray You'll use my weakness, failures, mistakes, pain, afflictions, and loss for Your glory. Thank You for developing me during my darkest times so I might help others. I ask You to reveal anyone in my life who needs Your comfort right now. Bring their face to my mind, I pray, and help me meet them with the very compassion You have given me. In Jesus's name we pray, Amen.

REFLECTION QUESTIONS

How do you typically view your afflictions? As random hardships with no purpose or as opportunities for development in compassion? How does today's passage speak to that view?

What about today's passage surprises you?

_____

_____

Who in your life needs comfort right now?

_____

_____

_____

_____

_____

_____

_____

_____

_____

_____

_____

_____

_____

_____

_____

_____

_____

_____

_____

_____

_____

_____

In what practical ways could you get uncomfortable in order to extend God's kindness and care to that person?

KIND IN BEARING BURDENS

KINDNESS // DAY 4

Yet it was kind of you to share my trouble.

PHILIPPIANS 4:14 (ESV)

So far this week, we've learned that God is kind, His kindness is more than a feeling (it *does* something—it changes us!), and His Spirit allows His kindness to flows through us toward others in the form of comfort.

What else does the Spirit's fruit of kindness look like as it works itself out in our lives? Paul gives us a hint in Philippians 4. As he writes a letter to the Philippian church, he makes it clear that ultimately, it is *Christ* who has helped him face seasons of prosperity and seasons of poverty. He claims boldly that in moments of abundance and in moments of need "it is Christ who strengthens me through it all!" (Phil. 4:13, paraphrased). And then, right after that, he tacks on our verse for today: "yet it was kind of you to share my trouble." Other translations say it this way:

> "Still, you did well by partnering with me in my hardship."

> "Even so, you have done well to share with me in my present difficulty" (NLT).

How amazing is that? Paul, the great apostle, who teaches us to find our ultimate strength in Christ during hard seasons—and who had miraculous personal encounters with Jesus—does not permit access to his struggles to Christ alone. He is willing to share his troubles not *just* with Jesus, but with his Philippian brothers and sisters too. His thanks for their kindness reveals that they were clearly intentional about bearing his burdens. These Philippians wanted to partner with him not only when it came to evangelism, missions, and financial needs, but also when it came to the messy, dark, burdensome parts of his life too!

Think about this. Paul could have easily said, "No, no. I'm fine! Christ is the strength I need! He can strengthen me through it all! You shouldn't extend a hand to me; you should allow me to trust Him all the more! After all, only Jesus has the power to deliver me from this trouble, or at least sustain me in it! Humans don't have the power for that, so I'm keeping my burdens at His feet, and His feet alone!" But he doesn't say that. He celebrates their kindness and leans into it—he says they've done the right thing to share in his troubles!

Why? Why would Paul, who knows Christ is the only One who is strong enough to bear the burden and the only One powerful enough to get him through his difficulty, be proud of the Philippians for jumping into his personal life and trying to help bear the load? Because they are acting like Christ! They are walking in the Savior's ways! After all, Jesus called others to Himself by offering to make their load lighter (Matt. 11:28–30). And now the Philippians are following His example, and making Paul's load lighter too. *The fruit in the Philippians' lives clearly looks like their Lord*, and Paul couldn't be happier about it!

If you're wondering what the fruit of kindness could look like in your life, or how it works itself out in your daily relationships, take a cue from the Philippian Christians—*kindness looks like sharing in the troubles of others*. Even when you can't fix it all. Even when you might only be able to take off a little bit of the load. Even when all you can offer is your presence, your prayer, or your pocketbook. After all, Jesus's example teaches us that if we allowed Him to serve us, we must serve each other in the same way! Or, as Jesus said: "For I have given you an example, that you also should do just as I have done to you" (John 13:15 ESV).

Let's commit to multiplying His kindness over everyone we have contact with and be His reflection. Let's show the world the burden-bearer our God is! Just imagine. We could become world-changers if we all did this in our daily lives!

PRAYER: Oh kind Father, thank You for not only being a safe place to bring my troubles, but for giving me another safe place in Your people! I pray You'll help me open myself up to the Christian brothers and sisters who are coming to mind right now. Give me the strength to allow them access into my struggles so we might bear them together. I pray also You'll bring to mind any burdens of others that You'd have me help carry. In doing so, develop me into a kind person—kind like Christ! Thank You for granting Your people—including me!—the opportunity to be more like Your Son, the greatest burden-bearer of all. Help me follow His example. Help me walk this earth just as He walked this earth, being kind to others. In Jesus's name, Amen.

REFLECTION QUESTIONS

Do you usually run toward those with big burdens, or do you usually shrink back? Why?

What about with your own burdens? Are you proud of other Christians for trying to help you, or do you shy away from letting them bear it alongside you? Why?

If you need to grow in receiving kindness, who might God want you to receive it from? Or, said another way, when it comes to your burdens and struggles and troubles right now, who in your life might God be leading you to permit access? How can you take a step toward granting them that access today?

On the flip side, if you need to grow in extending kindness, whose burdens might God be leading you to help carry? How can you take a step toward that today?

FORGIVING WHEN IT'S HARD

KINDNESS // DAY 5

Be kind to one another, tenderhearted, forgiving one another,
as God in Christ forgave you.

EPHESIANS 4:32 (ESV)

Have you ever found it hard to forgive? If you have a beating heart and breath in your lungs, the answer is most definitely yes! Forgiving is not easy, and for anyone who says it is, well, they may just be masking the pain until the point they can't anymore. Eventually, the wound someone else has inflicted will *hurt*.

Paul knew this very well. After all, he went through all sorts of things that required him to forgive others. He was beaten; he was mocked; he was run out of town over and over again for preaching the gospel! Many times he had to tend to *literal* wounds his enemies inflicted, and even then, he had to learn how to forgive. On top of these offenses from nonbelievers who hated his gospel ministry, he also faced *believers* who sinned against him too! Many times in his ministry, his brothers and sisters would either isolate away from him in fear, question him in skepticism, or outright attack his authority as an apostle in hatred.

It helps to know that a person who has been through *that* kind of stuff is the one writing our verse for today, am I right? It's the worst when you get advice for someone who really doesn't get it. But Paul? He gets it, friend!

So how can someone who's been through all those terrible things write "be kind to one another" or "be tenderhearted" or "forgive one another"? The answer is clear—because through Christ's sacrifice, God forgave *Paul* of terrible things! Paul knew he hurt God, and that God responded to that hurt by sending His own Son to pay for it. Paul knew forgiveness took sacrifice. And if forgiveness took sacrifice for God, it is going to take sacrifice for us too! It may hurt, but we can do it. Ultimately, Paul knew God's great formula: "Forgive as I have forgiven you."

Paul is clear. He leaves no room for excuse, even though we could find many because we sometimes like to hang on to our anger. Sometimes, we refuse to release our pain to God so that our hands might be open to reach out and forgive our neighbor. We dig our heels into the justifications we've made: "You don't know what they did to me." "They hurt me so bad." "They don't deserve to be forgiven." We never take the time to think of what our fate might be if Jesus had used the same logic with us instead of coming to pay for our sin and forgive us! We never stop to remember that these phrases weren't on Jesus's mouth when He paid for my sin and your sin, but instead "Forgive them for they don't know what they do."

God knows these things about us. He knows we'll be stubborn and dig our heels in and refuse to love when it is costly. He knows that in the intensity of our pain, we'll forget Christ's example. This is why He used Paul to remind us over and over again to stay tender, to release our wounds to God, and to be forgiving. Notice Paul says that these are all expressions of someone who is *kind*.

So what can we take from this? That the fruit of kindness in our lives, along with looking like comfort and burden-bearing, looks like *tenderness* and *forgiveness*. This means that if forgiveness doesn't show up in our lives all that often, well, *we can't call ourselves kind*. Whew! I don't know about you, but that's convicting for me!

There are many expressions of kindness in the Bible. But the type of kindness that *forgives* is clearly crucial to God. Why? Because relationships are important to Him, and without forgiveness, those relationships wouldn't stay together!

God's Word says that relationships are essential for us. They shape us—they are the environments in which God's virtues are developed in us. If we cut those relationships off, we can say bye-bye to our development as His followers! How else will the fruit of the Spirit be cultivated in us if we turn away from every single person who has done us wrong, in both big and small ways?

Think about it in terms of the Ten Commandments. This is so important to God that He places relationship with Himself and relationship with one another at the center of His first and second commandments! Given this, it should not be a surprise to us that relationships are the very means by which we are built up in the faith, even when it is difficult.

Friend, if you love God, then you must love His people and forgive them when they sin against you. This is how you go beyond head knowledge and get a real taste of all He went through to forgive you!

Through Christ, God was unbelievably kind to us. So let's live like we believe that, and be unbelievably kind to one another. Even when it means forgiving in a hard situation. After all, we left our old lives behind to be new creations. We began our life with Christ so that we might be different and act like children of God. We have to act like Christ, who laid down His life even when it cost Him! Who are we if we aren't kind like that?

In case you are starting to think this is easy for me, let me assure you: I had to learn this the hard way. For years, I wouldn't talk about the pain in my heart with anyone, especially when it came to my dad. It just brought up a bunch of anger, and I didn't want to feel like that. I could not understand why someone would choose an addiction instead of health, family, and kids. I couldn't wrap my head around someone who would abandon their family for a bad habit. The pain over my dad's decisions would always eat up my joy; it would keep me captive with a victim mentality—have you ever been there? Living in that prison cell never lets you see the other side of the story!

Eventually, as I grew in Christ, I realized that forgiveness wasn't optional. It was commanded. And so even on the days I was dying to understand—asking questions like *What on earth did I do to deserve this, God, and what on earth is he doing?!*—I ended my prayers by surrendering what I did not know with what I did know. I kept praying, even when I didn't feel much different afterward. I prayed for God to help me forgive. I prayed for His Spirit to give me the strength to release the pain into His hands, and let go of the resentment. I prayed for Him to take away my pride over how much better my new life was compared to my parents'. In those moments when I felt the temptation to dredge it all back up, I'd return over and over to the biblical reminders to forgive, and I'd say out loud, "I have forgiven them." For so long, I prayed this way.

You know what I came to find? That God is working on everyone in different ways. After years of asking for God to help me forgive, and choosing to forgive even when I didn't "feel" better, it was time to face the music. I got the chance to see my father one last time before his last stint in rehab. I traveled with my dad's sister to see him, and I remember knowing that this was it—when I laid eyes on my dad, God was going to reveal to me whether I had actually forgiven him or not. I remember thinking, *Forgiving a man like this isn't easy, but neither is it impossible, for with God, anything is possible!* Goodness, I remember the day as if it was yesterday. He walked toward me. I laid eyes on him. And I felt it rising up—compassion. *What on earth?* Compassion?! Yes, compassion. I had forgiven him. And I never want to forget that moment. I knew in an instant my Father in heaven didn't forget about me—He heard my cries and answered my prayer to be a forgiving person, even when it was costly.

Friend, *forgiven* shows *forgiveness*. It really is that simple. It's hard, but it's simple. It's hard, but it's possible. It's hard, but it's kind. Let's walk forward today, trusting God to produce this kind of "impossible" kindness in our lives and relationships. Because He can do it.

PRAYER: Oh Lord, I've said it and I'll say it again—thank You for Your forgiveness toward me. Thank You that Your kindness goes to the lengths of the cross! You know my failures, my every weakness, and You still forgive my trespasses over and over again. Thank You for being kind until it hurts, for my sake. Lord, help me grow here. Strengthen me to forgive! Help me extend kindness in this hard, but possible way. You know the faces coming to my mind right now—You know what they've done to me, and You know how hard it is for me to forgive. Help me be more like You! I can't do it on my own. I pray You'll give me the power to release the wounds to You and extend kindness instead of hate. Help me trust that You hear my prayer to be a forgiving person. Thank You for Your presence, Your Spirit, and Your Word, which can heal my deepest wounds. In Jesus's name, Amen.

REFLECTION QUESTIONS

Did you know that forgiveness was an expression of the fruit of kindness? How does this change your general view of kindness?

Who do you struggle most to forgive? Why?

_____

_____

_____

_____

_____

Briefly list the ways they've hurt you. Now, revisit the list. In what moments in your life have you been guilty of the same things (in big or small ways)?

_____

_____

_____

_____

_____

_____

_____

_____

_____

_____

_____

_____

_____

_____

_____

_____

How does Christ's example and Paul's example encourage you toward forgiveness today? How might you take a step toward forgiving someone this week?

_____

_____

_____

_____

_____

_____

REFLECTION AND REST

Use the last two days of this week to rest from reading, and instead, reflect on what you've learned. Use the journaling prompts and space below to process and enjoy what the Lord is doing in your heart.

1. What aspect of God's kindness did you find most encouraging this week? Most surprising?

2. In what tangible ways do you see the fruit of kindness being developed by God's Spirit in your heart and actions? Take some time to thank God for this fruitful work He's doing in you.

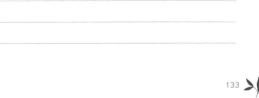

3. In this season of your life, which of these needs the most development in your heart? Circle one.

**A Kindness that Changes You.   Kind in Compassion and Comfort.
Kind in Bearing Burdens.   Forgiving When It's Hard.**

What are some practical next steps you can take to develop this?

_____

_____

_____

_____

_____

_____

_____

_____

_____

_____

FREESTYLE REFLECTION

Use this space below to pray, write out a meaningful passage of Scripture, or process anything God has placed on your heart this week.

GOD'S GOODNESS

GOODNESS // DAY 1

They celebrate your abundant goodness and
joyfully sing of your righteousness.

PSALM 145:7 (NIV)

One of my favorite things to do is celebrate. Whether it's Christmas, Thanksgiving, or birthdays, I just love a good reason to get together with those I love and cheer for something important. If you think about it, a celebration usually comes when something is done and finished and we can finally take some time to gather together and enjoy the close of a crazy season. For New Years, as an example, the year is finally finished, and we can say "cheers" to the completion of whatever it held. Or consider the finale of a Broadway musical when everyone rises to clap in a rowdy standing ovation—the practicing, rehearsing, and performance are finally finished, and the celebration functions as a sweet ending for everyone involved. These examples and many others are the sorts of celebrations we make a big deal out of, so why would we not do the same on a spiritual level?

In Psalm 145:7, the Bible tells us that God's people are doing just that—they are celebrating something spiritual. What, in particular, are they celebrating? God's goodness. And not just His goodness—His *abundant* goodness.

At this point we all nod along, don't we? *Yeah, yeah, yeah, God is good.* But what does that mean? If one of the fruits of the Spirit in our own heart is goodness, then that has to come from God first, right? We have to understand God as good before we can follow accordingly. *So what does it mean that God is good?* We use "good" in certain ways. We say, "Oh she's such a good girl." And what we mean is she's *nice*. So is that what God's goodness means? That He's *nice*? Or we say, "Oh man, that girlfriend of his is too good to him." What we mean is she *spoils* him, or treats his obvious wrongdoing in a permissive way. So is that what God is—permissive? Spoiling? Add in "abundant" to the equation and we have even more confusion. Is God *overly* nice? Too spoiling? Excessively permissive? *What in the world does good really mean?*

Thankfully, instead of trusting in our own ways of using the word *good*, if we look to the Bible, we are given an answer to this question!

First, God being good means that His character and judgments are morally pure. "The LORD is good and *upright*," Psalm 25:8 says, "Therefore he shows sinners the way" (emphasis added). There's a wrong way to go, and God shows us the good way, the morally right way. God's goodness is also equated to His provision and generosity. In Psalm 68:10, it says that God provides for the poor not just in His pity *but His goodness*. Other psalms also say that God's goodness is defined as His protection, His favor, His ability to satisfy, and His compassion (Pss. 84:11; 103:5; 145:9). Lastly, God's goodness is described by His commitment to remember us. The psalmist cries: "In keeping with your faithful love, remember me *because of your goodness*, LORD" (25:7, emphasis added).

> Friend, God helps you find the right way *because He's good.*
>
> God provides for you *because He's good.*
>
> God protects you *because He's good.*
>
> He gives you favor *because He's good.*
>
> He satisfies you and showers you with compassion *because He's good.*
>
> He remembers you, always, *because He's good.*

These things are what it means for God to be good to you. And they are what it means for us to be good as we walk according to His ways.

Have you seen these definitions of God's goodness in your life? Have you seen evidence of His goodness raining down on your life? Celebrate it!

Heaven knows I've seen His goodness in my life. Even in seasons I would have given anything to change my circumstances, I can see evidence of His goodness. Even through the addiction issues that ran in my family, He taught me the right way to go. He gave me the wisdom not to follow in their footsteps. He saved me from going back to the same pit they fell into. He helped me find the way not toward addiction, repeating the cycle, but away from it, on a path toward health and life! And then

His good provision? What can I say? His goodness provided for my day-to-day needs as I trusted Him. People came pouring in my life who would share their resources, and God would provide bus coupons, shoes for running, hand-me-downs, rides to school and events. Through others in my family and greater community, God always found ways to bless me. And His protection? I can't tell you how many times I can look back and see that He protected me in my own childhood wounds, and even in my new family now with my husband and kids. God protects us all the time, even when it's difficult. We have seen His favor poured out when we didn't deserve it, when there was no way and many of those around us either didn't understand us or were against us. His compassion met us in hard places, and He remembered us every step of the way. When we define goodness the way the Bible does, we cannot say anything but this: God is good to us.

Friend, we can all celebrate God's goodness in our present for the past, can't we? Even if we face a current season when our prayers are not being answered, and we are waiting for His time to be revealed, or we are in deep external or internal pain, we can remember times He's been good. And we can exercise faith to believe He'll be good to us again. Even if it's for something as simple as the food on our table, clean water, or a bed to sleep in, we've seen the good hand of God helping us in this life. Even in the wait or in pain, He is good—not just when we notice, but also when we don't. His goodness is *who He is* and that cannot be changed. That means His goodness never ends—it is not done with you yet!

We should celebrate His abundant goodness in our lives not just because it's good to do as His children (Matt. 7:11), but because it's good for *our* children to witness in our lives. Our celebrations teach our kids what is worth cheering for in this life, and what is worth forgetting, or putting in the background. How will they learn to see God's goodness if we don't celebrate it in our own lives? After all, His abundant goodness does not stop with us; it keeps rolling over down to the next generation. So don't let His goodness be forgotten or taken for granted in your family or your home. Let the stories of His goodness keep giving life and hope to the generation after you. Tell your kids (or children in your life) about prayers answered just as you prayed they would, and also prayers answered in ways you didn't expect, for all of these experiences sing of God's goodness in our lives. Celebrate how abundant God's goodness was in those memories in your story, and teach the children around you to celebrate their own moments of His good work in their lives too.

How, you may ask? I take every chance to remind my children how blessed they are right now. They have so much more than what my husband and I grew up with. I remind them that God has given them a safe home, stable parents, provided them with what they need daily, and abundantly more to share. I talk about the needs we faced when we were kids, and how the Lord has shown up in our lives. Even in the necessities of life, He also took care of our hearts. I tell them how He had always provided abundantly with His presence and protection. I pass down the stories of when I didn't have a home, and how family members and friends took me in. I let them listen to the tale of those times I was lacking a father-figure, and God gave me *three* father-figures to guide me in my early adult years! I share about the ways my godfather invested in me spiritually in college, pointing me back to Jesus, teaching me the Word, and helping me see that at the end of the day, God was the Father that I always wanted and needed. In moments they feel like life is moving too slow, I tell them the stories of how God's timing was confusing for me in certain seasons, but then, looking back later, I now see how His timing was perfect. Or when it comes to prayer, I remind them that God's will is good. Even if they are praying for something nonstop and not getting it, *it's okay*, because we'd rather be in God's will than out of it. Or when it comes to getting hurt in life, I remind them that in God's goodness, He doesn't allow harm so deep that He cannot heal it. Though the sin of others makes terrible things happen, He turns them for good, and He always has a better comeback than evil. His goodness can overcome any sin, and always protects the greater purpose of our pain; His goodness always prevails. I remind them in my own life, if I lacked anything or anybody, God always, somehow, gave me a double or triple portion in some way I couldn't expect. I remind them, I remind them, I remind them.

In short, I certainly don't do it perfectly, but I try as hard as I can to tell my children of the goodness of God. As much as we hate reminding them or feeling like a broken record, the truth is, *they really need it*. The next generation needs to hear that God is good. They need the stories. They need the reminder just as much as you and I do!

Remember how celebrations put a sweet ending on something that is finally finished? I want to encourage you: the greatest reminder of God's goodness for yourself and for your kids—and for anyone you encounter in this life—is the reminder of what Jesus has done for you on the cross. Celebrating that makes all the sense in the world because the work of Jesus guarantees us *it is finished*. Our God said our sin and our once-terrible future was finished and done with. In Him, we now have no more sin to pay for and a future that is secure! We no longer need constant payment for sin—His blood was enough! All the other evidence of God's goodness are reasons to celebrate and shout, but the gospel? It's the greatest of them all!

Friend, when we consider the big and small signs of God's goodness in our lives, especially the cross, we can't help but realize that we serve and celebrate a God whose fidelity and goodness has no limits. He is the One who gives and keeps giving. We didn't do anything to deserve His goodness, but we can bank on the fact that it will be there to meet us every morning, and we'll always have a story to tell about it.

And so my prayer for you and me both today is that we will sing as loud as we can so anyone who hears us will know His goodness toward those who love Him. My hope is that you'll never stop joining this celebration—that you'll never keep God's goodness to yourself and you'll never stop telling of His abundant wonders in your life.

And more than that, I hope His very goodness will bear itself out in your life. That it won't be something you just celebrate, but a fruit of His Spirit that works itself out in your heart and your daily actions—that you'll follow His goodness and live in light of it. I pray you'll share it with others, and your heart and actions will be good too. That like God, you'll be set on walking the right way and you'll be a provisional figure in someone else's life. Like God, I hope you'll be protective over someone who is vulnerable or defenseless—that you'll give favor to those who don't deserve it, you'll shower others with compassion, and you'll remember those who are often forgotten.

This is goodness. This is what we get to experience from God Himself. This is what we get to pass down to our children. And this is what we get to live out in daily life, no matter who we encounter. And *that is* worth celebrating, friend.

PRAYER: Dear Lord, thank You for being a God who is fully and truly good, and who loves me without limits! Help me believe You are good in the seasons I am tempted to believe You are not. Open my eyes to the ways You have been upright—to the ways You have provided for me, protected me, satisfied me, poured out compassion on me, remembered me, and granted me favor. Help me celebrate these stories with those around me, especially the next generation. Help me leave behind any ways that are not good, and adopt Your good ways in my life. Reveal to me any chance I can praise You for Your abundant goodness "so that all people may know of your mighty acts and the glorious splendor of your kingdom" (Ps. 145:12 NIV). Thank You for doing everything needed for me to know You—for finishing the job on the cross and leaving nothing for me but Your goodness! Help me live like this is true, and be good to others like You are. And use my life and my stories so the next generation can do the same! In Jesus's name, Amen.

REFLECTION QUESTIONS

What are some typical ways our world defines "good"? In what ways is the Bible's definition of *good* different than the worlds?

How have you seen God prove Himself upright, a provider, a protector, a giver of favor, a satisfier, a compassionate Father, and One who remembers you?

_____

_____

_____

_____

_____

What stories of God's goodness can you share with your children (or kids in your life) this week? How can you practically celebrate God's goodness in your family?

_____

_____

_____

_____

_____

_____

_____

_____

_____

_____

_____

_____

_____

_____

_____

_____

_____

In your own words, explain how the cross of Christ is the greatest display of God's goodness.

_____

_____

_____

THE FRUIT OF GOODNESS GROWS OVER TIME

GOODNESS // DAY 2

And I am sure of this, that he who began a good work in you
will bring it to completion at the day of Jesus Christ.

PHILIPPIANS 1:6 (ESV)

As we saw yesterday, we know God is good. He does good things because He *is* good, deep down to the core. Said another way, His actions are good because His *nature* is good.

But what about us? Are we like this too? Are we *good* all the way through, like God is?

The Scriptures start by saying yes, and then they veer into a very clear *no*.

In the beginning, God made the world and humans good. In fact, while He calls all the other parts of His creation "good," He calls humans "very good" (Gen. 1). So, there's part of our answer: yes, we started off good! That's how we were originally built. *Very good!*

But then came something terrible. After Adam and Eve rebelled against God, sin and suffering infected not only them, but the whole world, and every human who was born after them. This moment—the one when sin entered the world—is called "the Fall."

And so since that day, every human who came into the world after the Fall, including you and me, was born with an internal nature that is bent toward sin, which means *not good*. Romans 3:10–12 (ESV) would put it this way: "None is righteous, no, not one; no one understands; no one seeks for God. All have turned aside; together they have become worthless; no one does good, not even one." (See also Pss. 14:1–3; 53:1–3; and Eccles. 7:20.)

To sum it up, although we all are still born with inherent worth and dignity because we bear the image of God, because of the sin that lives inside of us all, we went from *very good* to *not good*.

These are not words we like to hear, are they? But at the end of the day, we kinda know it's true. We are capable of good things, but we see ourselves do all sorts of things that aren't good. We snap at our spouses, we're harsh with our kids, we lie, we cheat, we steal, in big and small ways. We harbor anger and bitterness and jealousy. Just looking at the state of the world right now can tell us pretty quickly that humans aren't perfectly good all the way through.

So what is our hope? Will we remain "not good" forever?

The Scriptures give an equally strong answer here: *no*, we won't remain like this forever! Because of the power of Jesus's saving blood, we are new creations! And after becoming new creations in conversion, we are given the Holy Spirit, who slowly makes us more like Jesus over time. We have a ways to go, but our hope is that God's Spirit, over time, makes us more and more *good*, like God. He restores us back to the design of "very good" we were always built for!

Isn't that great news? God is able to make you and me "very good" again. And not just on the action level, but the nature level. He can make us good on the inside so we do good things on the outside. He will help goodness grow in us over time!

That's what our verse for today is all about. God has begun a good work in us, and He will complete it in us over time. We have confidence that He has a purpose for us from the beginning in Genesis to the end of Revelation. Just think about it: in every book of the Scriptures, He has started His mission and He has also finished it, as His plans unfold all the way to the cross, the resurrection, and finally, the new heavens and new earth. *He will finish the big story of the Bible. It is His master plan, and He won't give up on it.* And if he will finish something that big, we can be sure He'll finish little old *us*! That includes bearing all sorts of fruit in us, including goodness, which will abide in us as we abide in Him. Praise be to Him—our God finishes what He starts! There is no one like our God.

I've had to learn this very lesson during the writing process of the book you hold in your hands right now. Trusting His process has taken me a while. I wondered, *Why are You so gracious to me, God, to let me do things I am insecure about, or feel incapable of doing?* I wrestled with the idea that He would use me for anything good in this world because many times, I feel discouraged about my shortcomings and all the knowledge I have yet to gain. In those moments, He has reminded me of His provision and goodness in my salvation. And if He was provisional and good to me in my salvation moment, He must be good to me in every moment that follows! He helped me see I was never alone!

Friend, you are never alone. God has been good to you in your past, and whatever He might be calling you to in this season, His goodness will follow you there too! Don't let anything keep you from growing in your understanding of His goodness. He alone has done great things in your life, and He is currently at work in it. Whatever it is you feel insecure about inside—some spiritual shortcoming or area of growth you need help in—know that He *will* complete it according to His will and His perfect timing. He is at work today, tomorrow, and always.

How has He been good to you when you were "not good"? How has he continued to develop goodness in your heart, even when you were plagued with past memories of your own unworthiness or unfaithfulness? Think of a memory, even now, and worship Him for it!

What comes to mind for me is this: I still remember the days I called myself a Christian, but I was Christless. I didn't trust in His sacrifice for me, and I wasn't seeking Him or searching to really know Him until, like I've shared before, my desperation took me to dedication. I was empty and hungry, though I claimed to be full and satisfied. I tried to bear the name of our Savior to save face, but did not actually walk with Him. Thank God He was kind and good to reveal Himself to me. He knew me and He knew my heart. He knew all of my sin, all of my *not-good-ness, and He opened my eyes to the gospel anyway*! His goodness pointed out my weakness and that was what I needed.

God knew all the places I was "not good." He knew exactly where to start with me, and He knows exactly how to start with you. He knows exactly where you are and knows what you need when you need it.

I look back now, and can't believe the journey. I still have so far to go, but where I was once a girl stuffed full of selfishness, now I can genuinely see God has started to produce true goodness in me. It's not a completed project yet, trust me! *I have my days*, friend (you know what I mean). But I can see in fits and spurts, slowly but surely, that He's moving me back to "very good" again. He's making me more like Jesus! And He's doing the same with you too. He will not give up on you because you feel unfinished or incomplete. He has started a good work in you, and He will also finish it!

PRAYER: Oh Lord and Savior of my soul, You've been nothing but good to me! More than that, You are committed to developing goodness in me from the beginning to the end of my journey. You won't stop until You see the good work You've started in me come to completion! You are the God who takes "not good" and makes it "very good." Do it in me, today! Refresh me with Your presence today, and help me walk in Your good ways. In Jesus's name, Amen.

REFLECTION QUESTIONS

In your own words, explain what changed humans from "very good" to "not good"?

In your own words, explain what changes humans back from "not good" to "very good" again?

_____

in what ways do you see
God growing goodness
in you over time?

_____

_____

_____

_____

_____

_____

_____

_____

_____

_____

_____

_____

_____

_____

_____

_____

_____

_____

_____

_____

_____

_____

_____

When you are
tempted to believe
the lie that God won't
finish the good work He started
in you, what practical things can you
do to help yourself remember the truth?

WHAT GOODNESS REALLY LOOKS LIKE

GOODNESS // DAY 3

Mankind, he has told each of you what is good,
and what it is the LORD requires of you:
to act justly, to love faithfulness, and to walk humbly with your God.

MICAH 6:8

What comes naturally to you? Singing? Painting? Interior design? Running? *Shopping* (ha!)? When we look at Scripture, we can easily see that God is "a natural" at goodness because that is His character. As James 1:17 says, "Every good and perfect gift is from above, coming down from the Father of lights, who does not change like shifting shadows." God is completely good, all the way through! There is no "shifting shadow" in Him.

As we explored yesterday, none of us are "naturals" at goodness because of sin. Yet God is bearing that fruit in us day by day, helping goodness *become* more natural. It may take time, but God is committed to this—He *will* develop goodness in us! So, how do we know when God is developing more goodness within us? In what ways is this fruit of goodness identified in our lives, so that we'll know it when we see it? What does the fruit of goodness really look like in everyday moments? How can we learn to identify it, so we can participate in our growth, cultivating goodness as it goes from seed, to seedling, to full-on bloom?

Micah 6:8 helps us answer these questions! Micah helps us move from seeing goodness in a nice, vague way to viewing it in a "brass tacks" way. He shows us what goodness looks like, according to God. He says it point blank: "God has told each of you what is good."

If you have kids, join along with me in saying this: WE FEEL YOU, MICAH! How many times do we raise our mama-voices across the house when we hear the ruckus—"Little wild ones, don't you act like you don't know the deal! I've *told* you what you're supposed to do—in fact, I've told *each one* of you! You know what it is to be good to each other; don't act like you don't know, child!"

When we look at Micah 6:8, it's clear *we're* the kids in the situation, am I right? God has told us—*each and every one of us*—what goodness looks like. But like our kids, we get caught up in our daily squabbles and stressors, and we forget. And in His goodness, God goes on to remind us again that goodness looks like:

- *acting justly:* doing the **right thing**, no matter what.

- *loving faithfulness:* having a stubborn love for all people, and desiring **mercy and kindness** for both our friends and our enemies!

- *walking humbly with God:* going about every single day sticking close to God's side, receiving His love and awaiting His direction, because we know that **He is God, and we are not!**

Do some of these seem hard to pull off at the same time? You're right—they do! For example, think about God's call for us to be both *just* and *merciful*. Micah isn't the only prophet God uses to communicate how important these two things are. Remember Hosea saying something similar in Hosea 12:6? "But you must return to your God. Maintain love and justice, and always put your hope in God." Mercy and justice are two pillars God consistently asked His people to live by, because they are two foundational things that are true about *Him*. There are two things that make *Him* good. And God mentions them side by side for a reason—they go better together than separate! Let me tell you why.

If we take them separately, then we'd live by one or the other instead of both, and we'd be terribly imbalanced. If we only practiced mercy, we would allow for wrongdoings all the time, and no evil would get corrected. But if we were only just, we'd only be hammering all the wrongdoing of other people and we'd be cold and cruel. We wouldn't remember that every believer is at a different spiritual level, and we wouldn't be able to correct them in the warmth of brotherly love. Mercy without justice doesn't point to Jesus! It would just leave everyone in sin with nowhere to go but eternal punishment. Justice without mercy doesn't point to Jesus either! It can get the score settled, but it would squash the sinner and leave no room for the warmth of relationship after the sins are dealt with. In the end, being a "good" person doesn't mean being a just person *or* a merciful person. It means being a person who walks in both justice and mercy.

You're probably thinking what I'm thinking when I see justice, mercy, and humility listed out as the definition of goodness: it looks like Jesus! And you're right: Jesus was good in all these ways. And if we're found in Him and He is found in us, we will reflect His goodness in our Christian walk.

Though we often forget what goodness looks like on a daily basis, isn't it helpful to know that God reminds us? He doesn't leave it up to our imagination to figure out if we're being "good." If left to ourselves, we'd probably define it in all sorts of wrong ways! We'd all probably assume we were good people simply because we were praised by people we admire, or we got all our work done for this week at our job, or we got an A on a test at school. But you can do all three of those things and still not be good, according to God! Thankfully, He's told us how to identify the fruit of goodness in our lives. If we see one of these three things flowing out of our heart and into our daily life, true goodness is growing! So, friend, let's cultivate these things in our lives together today!

How, you might ask? To cultivate these things is not always easy. Take humility, for example. To be humble is difficult, yes, but not impossible! We can cultivate humbleness in our everyday life by coming to Christ honestly at the beginning of each day. We can bring the real us into His presence —the UNFILTERED us!—and in that place of mess, we can receive His strength and His help and remember that we are yet loved by Him. He knows our hearts and our intentions. He knows the patchy places where goodness needs to grow. And by His Spirit, He can provide that goodness in exactly the measure we need it! He can provide whatever it is we lack, whether it is mercy or justice or anything else! It all starts with being unfiltered and honest with Him—there's no way you can be these things before Christ and not grow in goodness!

So I'll say it again: let's push past our fear, come to Christ unfiltered, and cultivate these things in our lives. Then we can become good like our Savior is! As I often tell myself, "Every good thing comes from God, and everything else He has the power to change!"

PRAYER: Oh Father, I come before You now and bring all my mess! No filters! You know the issues I bring to You, and the ways I have not aligned with Your definition of goodness. I stop right now and worship Your character—You are truly and fully good! You are in the highest place, and yet You share with me Your justice, mercy, and love. Grow me in goodness, I pray, especially in the area I am weakest. You know the patchy places in my heart that need to be cultivated so they can finally blossom into something that looks more like Jesus. Your heart for the world is good—develop the same heart in me! Help me reflect Your goodness to others so they can find Your goodness in their lives too. In Jesus's name, Amen.

REFLECTION QUESTIONS

When you assume someone is a "good person," what evidence do you typically give? Look at the evidence you listed as proof that someone is "good." Is it the same as God's definition of *good*, as revealed in Micah 6:8? Why?

Circle which part of God's definition is hardest for you? Why do you think this is the case? How might you take a step toward cultivating this aspect of goodness?

mercy   justice   humility

_____

_____

**What holds you back from coming
to Christ in an unfiltered way?
How could this practice
grow you in
humility?**

_____

_____

_____

_____

_____

_____

_____

_____

_____

_____

_____

_____

_____

_____

_____

_____

_____

_____

_____

_____

_____

_____

_____

_____

_____

**How have you
seen God grow you
in the areas of mercy,
justice, or humility in the
last few years?**

_____

_____

_____

NOT GROWING WEARY IN THE GOOD RACE

GOODNESS // DAY 4

But as for you, brothers and sisters,
do not grow weary in doing good.

2 THESSALONIANS 3:13

Have you ever been just *bone*-tired? Weary? I know I have. Running around after kiddos, being a wife, serving my church, overseeing the Fruitful Girl ministry—there are days it feels like I just can't catch a breath. It's hard work. But you know what? Of all the work I could be doing, it's *good* work too.

One thing I love about our verse for today is that it assumes good work gets tiring some days! The Bible doesn't sugarcoat things. It tells the truth. It gets real. And the real truth is good work is both meaningful and hard. When you're living in a world turned toward badness, working hard toward *goodness* feels super uphill sometimes, am I right? God knows this. He acknowledges this sort of thing that gets us weary sometimes.

Marriage and ministry and parenting are one thing. We know the long-term effects of those moments if we stay the good course. But what about those times we *can't* see the long-term effects? What about those random moments that have no obvious connection to our lives? Like those times someone cuts us off so quick in traffic that our life flashes before our eyes? Or the moments people don't use their blinkers to merge onto the freeway or the times someone is randomly rude to us at the store? What about those times when we share a well-meaning social media post, and the angry comments come darting toward us like sharp, hurtful daggers? What about when someone slanders us or misunderstands us in front of everybody else at that gathering (a work meeting, PTA meeting, a church gathering, or otherwise)? What about when that customer service representative makes us tell the story *twenty different times* before they'll finally give us a refund (that is, if they'll even actually give it to us!)? What about when our neighbor points out that *one* dead patch of grass in our yard for the third summer in a row? What about when someone we looked up to lets us down?

Full transparency: I still need *a lot* of grace to remain genuinely good in those situations. And I have a feeling you might need the same! So how do we do it? We know God is good, and we know we're supposed to bear the fruit of goodness, even in those exhausting/maddening moments. So how do we keep at it? How can we not grow weary in doing good?

To answer that, allow me to share a little story from my tender high school years. I'll never forget it. It was my junior year, during a race, and our track coach told my team he would no longer be coaching us. I was so upset! I loved my coach, and given how hard my family life was with my own parents, I probably took this departure worse than others on my team. He had become such a role model for me, and one of the only healthy adults I trusted. I cried. And I also had a plan.

My plan was to intentionally lose the race, give up, and make my coach watch me come in last place. (Nothing wrong with coming in last place, by the way, so long as you're not doing it on purpose!) *That'll show him!* I thought. My teammates and I always used to win every race with 1st, 2nd, and 3rd places, so I knew this would come as a shock to him. When it was time to start, I ran normally, but within a lap or so, I started to relax and decrease my pace. I was in the second lap of the 2-mile race and doing very well, but then I hung back and eventually slowed down to seventh, eighth, and then ninth place, other runners bolting ahead of me. It was then I heard a familiar voice. (If you are a runner or swimmer, you know that in a race, you don't listen to anybody else other than your coach because you develop something called not only *tunnel vision*, but also *tunnel hearing*. This means only selected and familiar voices can enter the tunnel, and you respond to them like your life depends on it!) You probably already know who the voice was: my coach who had just quit on us before the race!

He looked at me. "Are you okay?"

My answer rang out loud and clear. "NO!"

Clearly, in his view, I was fine. No injuries or issues. So he said, "Okay, pick it up, Yahaira!"

"NO!"

"Don't give up; you can still catch up!" he tried to reason.

"No, no, no!"

As adults we now have a radar for what's going on with kids. But at the time, I was surprised my coach figured it out. He realized I was upset because he wasn't going to coach us anymore. And you know what? He knew *exactly* what to tell me to help me catch up, and enter back in the race with renewed determination.

"Yahaira, I'm not leaving right this minute! I'm gonna keep coaching you until the end of the season. *I'm finishing the season with all of you!* Now go and win it!"

I remember moving so fast after hearing those words. Even after feeling so weary! Knowing he would still be there for the rest of the season changed everything. It gave me the energy, resolve, determination, and boost I needed to jump back in and give it my all. I worked really hard and put in everything I had. After a hard, long push and feet flying over the track, I ended up in second place! My teammates and I got 1st, 2nd, and 3rd place as a group, just as we normally did.

Two things got me through that tough moment. One, *tunnel hearing*. When all seemed too hard, I still let the right voice speak to me. Even when I was confused and stubborn and frustrated and screaming, I was still able to engage in the conversation with my coach because I had developed the ability to let his voice reach me—even when he was the one I was mad at! Two, knowledge that my coach was going to be by my side for the whole season. He wasn't up and leaving. He was staying until the end of that stretch of time we needed him most. He was there in *this* moment when I needed him, and he was going to be there on the other side, at *that* ending moment of the season.

The point of my story is this: you'll have the choice to give up in certain stretches of life. You'll get weary in running your race and you'll get tired of doing good when it seems like there's no immediate reward. In those moments, don't let the circumstances stop you from running a good race. Don't let other people's decisions or actions take away from your good. Turn off all those voices in your head and apply tunnel hearing— listen only to the voice of God as revealed in His Word. He'll help energize you when you're weary! And remember, He's here right now with you, in the hard moment, and He's *also* waiting for you on the other end of this season called life.

God is good to us all the time. We're called to "hold on to what is good" (1 Thess. 5:21). So hold on to the good voice of God now, and also trust in the truth that you'll enjoy His presence forever on the other side. He has not abandoned you! Let that rich truth help you get back up, get back in the game, and run as fast as you can toward doing good. Don't worry about the beginning of the race, or the parts that got hard. Even if you feel discouraged, what matters is the end of the race. Don't give up before finishing. Don't grow weary in doing good because you have a God who will help you and coach you all the way through!

PRAYER: Heavenly Father, thank You for Your goodness over me, in me, and around me! I pray today that You'd help me remember the good things You've called me to do. If I've put myself on the sidelines, help me get back in the game by hearing Your voice! Thank You for teaching me that if I'm living out Your goodness in this world, I can't lose, no matter how slow or weary it may feel in the hard moments. I pray You'll help me continue the good race by Your strength and help—I know You can help me finish stronger than ever! Thank You for Your promises and Your presence that encourages me not to give up but to keep up doing good in a world gone wrong. In Jesus's name, Amen.

REFLECTION QUESTIONS

What particular situations most tempt you to stop doing good? Why?

When it comes to good things that God has called you to do, are there any you've given up doing because it feels too wearisome? What are they?

_____
_____
_____
_____
_____

What voices do you allow to "coach" you in really hard moments? Is God's voice the loudest? Why or why not? As it relates to God's voice, how might you develop better "tunnel hearing"?

_____
_____
_____
_____
_____
_____
_____
_____
_____
_____
_____
_____
_____
_____
_____
_____
_____
_____
_____
_____

How does it feel to remember God is with you every stretch of this season of life, and also on the other side of it?

GOOD WORKS

GOODNESS // DAY 5

For we are his workmanship, created in Christ Jesus for good works, which God prepared beforehand, that we should walk in them.

EPHESIANS 2:10 (ESV)

I used to think good works were the sole responsibility of Christians while God sat back with His feet up. Like He wound up the clock of this world and then just let it go, letting things unfold however they were going to unfold, basically leaving us to figure it out if something went wrong . As if His work was done in creating us, and then it was on us to get to work from that point on. But this couldn't be further from the truth.

God isn't sitting back, hands off the world. God's goodness is still at work right now! He's involved. He's working. Metaphorically speaking, He's still got His hands moving and shaping and laboring. Wondering how this is true? Or what exactly, He's up to as He works in the world? Concentrate on this part of our verse today: *We* are His workmanship. If you're wondering what God's up to these days, or what His good work looks like, the answer is *you and me*! The answer is His global church! *We* are His masterpiece, His sculpture, His art project, the thing He's working on every single day until His Kingdom comes. In Christ, He forms and shapes us into the people we're supposed to be like.

And what, exactly, are we supposed to be like? We're supposed to be like Him! And so if He's up to good work, then we should be up to good work too, right? In fact, there are good works that He has specifically prepared for us to do before we even knew about it. We go about our days up to good work because *He* is up to good work, and we want to reflect Him.

It's important to stop and make clear that good works do not save us. Instead, they are simply what we do in response to a loving God who, in His goodness, came and saved us. If we were a tree, the root would be our faith and salvation, accomplished by the work of Jesus Christ, and our good works are the fruit that our faith and salvation produce. We are not productive in order to be saved. Instead, *because* we are saved, we bear the fruit of good works so that we might look more like God and help the world around us flourish. If there is zero fruit of good works, well then, the tree is probably dead! Or, as the book of James would put it, faith by itself without good works as fruitful evidence of salvation is dead (James 2:17).

I used to be like that dead tree. As I've said before, I once called myself a Christian for years, yet my "tree" never produced real fruit. When I realized this, it was heart-shattering, but my God was faithful to me. When I realized my life had to bear fruit for His glory, that shifted how I read things and saw things. When I realized I could only change myself with His help and shower myself with His goodness, the "works" in my life really started to change.

If you feel that way today—if you have a sneaking suspicion you're not really *living* like a Christian even though you may have always *identified* as one—let me share something with you. Let me share what I did to better reflect God's goodness in our world and finally be ready for any good work He had prepared for me to do:

> 1. **Confess what's been holding you back.** For me, if I had an unconfessed sin that was holding me back, I found if I brought it into the light and dealt with it before God directly, a weight was lifted off. After confessing sin, I found I was a much cleaner "instrument" for God's service. Every instrument is better after the gunk is cleaned out! I encourage you to confess and forsake sin at the time you realize it and not wait for tomorrow.

> 2. **Forgive.** I realized another thing holding me back from bearing fruit was unforgiveness. I had to forgive not just others, but myself too! Forgiving others includes those who hurt you or made your life a bit more complicated than it had to be. I know it's hard to let go of those past wounds. But I encourage you to let it go and ask the Lord to help you release yourself from your jail cell. He will! Friend, unforgiveness can hold us back from spiritual growth. Forgiven people must forgive others, and built-up unforgiveness is another thing that clogs an instrument. Clean it out! The Lord will take care of the pain.

3. **Seek the Lord consistently.** I used to be a person who only remembered the Lord in the hard times, when I needed something from Him, or during Christian holidays like Christmas or Easter. The Bible tells us this is not the same thing as a real relationship with God! Think about it—do you like when a person only reaches out to you when they need something? Of course not. Then why would God? Seek the Lord in the good season and in the bad, continually and consistently. Walk with Him all your days, not just some of them. It's so much richer when you do this!

4. **Get out of starvation mode.** Our bodies go into starvation mode when we don't nourish it properly, on a daily basis. If we only eat two days a week, for example, we aren't dieting, we're starving ourselves. This is true spiritually too. I used to be a "starving Christian." Meaning, I'd only "eat" the Word of God on Sundays, and I'd starve until next Sunday. I was not reading or studying the Bible daily for myself. I'd just let someone else feast on God's Word, and then share with me what the meal was like later. They'd digest the Word for themselves and then regurgitate it to me. What I didn't realize is that God wanted me to consume the Word for myself! He didn't want me feasting on someone else's meal. He wanted to give me my own! Jump into the Word of God daily, friend. You need this daily bread! And as a perk, guess what? Learning Scripture ends up helping you discern the will of God and make better decisions!

5. **Pray.** Before truly coming to Christ, I was a prayerless believer. I only prayed when I desperately needed a fix to a big problem. Like we've said before, a relationship requires more than just connection over crisis moments. If this sounds like you, spend time in prayer daily and, most importantly, pray for others. I started praying for others, and that helped me learn how to pray on an everyday basis. Look up the Lord's Prayer too, and follow along to get you started.

6. **Join a church.** The church is the family of God. Joining Christ and walking in good works is something the whole church does together—not something you do on your own! So join a church that teaches the Bible and treats it as

authoritative and helpful for all of life. I remember the first time I volunteered at my church. I joined a Bible study, and they announced they needed volunteers in the video room. I knew nothing about a video room. Well, I became a camera operator! I had no idea how to use it, but I was trained by others who served at the church, and I enjoyed that for years until the Lord called me to lead a Bible study group. Step into the family of God, friend. You have brothers and sisters waiting to walk with Him and serve by your side! Jump in by faith, and with an open heart to serve Him, God will prepare you for so many good works!

God's good works are you and me, friend. He is tending to the fruit He is cultivating in each one of us, including the fruit of goodness. As He pours His goodness into our hearts and lives, we then overflow in that goodness and respond by walking in good works toward others. God is up to good things! He's working. Let's join Him!

PRAYER: Heavenly Father, how in the world is it possible that I am Your good work, along with the rest of Your church? Thank You for making us Your masterpiece! You know whether or not I'm reflecting this part of Your character today. You know whether or not I'm walking in good works. Help me develop into a better instrument to be used for Your service. Clean out any build-up that has been clogging me spiritually, and connect me with a spiritual family You want me to join and serve. Help me have eyes to see the good works You have prepared for me to do, and give me the strength to do them by Your power and in Your name. Thank You for including me in Your great plans and giving me the opportunity to reflect Your goodness in this world. In Jesus's name, Amen.

REFLECTION QUESTIONS

**Have you ever thought that
God was no longer working
in His world? That He was
uninvolved? How does
today's verse speak
to this?**

**Do you
identify as
a Christian? How
does that differ from
living like a Christian?**

_____

_____

_____

_____

_____

**Are you walking in good works today?
If not, what's holding you back?
Of the list mentioned, which
item is hardest
for you? Why?**

_____

_____

_____

_____

_____

_____

_____

_____

_____

_____

_____

_____

_____

_____

_____

_____

_____

_____

_____

_____

_____

_____

**What local church
or place of service might
God be asking you to step
toward in this season of life?**

_____

_____

_____

REFLECTION AND REST

Use the last two days of this week to rest from reading, and instead, reflect on what you've learned. Use the journaling prompts and space below to process and enjoy what the Lord is doing in your heart.

1. What aspect of God's goodness did you find most encouraging this week? Most surprising?

_____

_____

_____

_____

_____

_____

_____

_____

2. In what tangible ways do you see the fruit of goodness being developed by God's Spirit in your heart and actions? Take some time to thank God for this fruitful work He's doing in you.

_____

_____

_____

_____

_____

_____

_____

_____

3. In this season of your life, which of these needs the most development in your heart? Circle one.

Understanding that Goodness Grows over Time.
Expressing Goodness through Mercy, Justice, and Humility.
Not Growing Weary in Running the Good Race.   Continuing in Good Works.

What are some practical next steps you can take to develop this?

_____

_____

_____

_____

_____

_____

_____

_____

_____

_____

FREESTYLE REFLECTION

Use this space below to pray, write out a meaningful passage of Scripture, or process anything God has placed on your heart this week.

GOD'S FAITHFULNESS

FAITHFULNESS // DAY 1

For we are his workmanship, created in Christ Jesus for good works, which God prepared beforehand, that we should walk in them.

EPHESIANS 2:10 (ESV)

As it is with every fruit of the Spirit, we cannot think about being faithful in our daily lives without first realizing where the fruit of faithfulness comes from: God! God's Spirit produces in us what's already present in *Him*, and that includes faithfulness.

God's faithfulness . . . where to begin? I suppose the right answer is the beginning, because He has been faithful from the start of Genesis to the end of Revelation. If we look through the story of Scripture, we see it on every page. God was faithful to provide for Adam and Eve in the garden. And even when they rebelled against Him, He made a promise to save them from their sin, and He kept that promise. Faithful!

One wonderful passage that gets at God's faithfulness is found in the book of Joshua:

> "You know with all your heart and all your soul that
> none of the good promises the LORD your God made
> to you has failed. Everything was fulfilled for you;
> not one promise has failed." (Josh. 23:14)

As Joshua reminds us, the Lord has been faithful to us through all of His promises. Not one thing God has promised in His Word has failed to come through! In fact, did you know that all the promises of God recorded in Scripture can be considered fulfilled in Jesus Christ? He is the rescuer God promised; He is the divine presence we need; He's the sacrifice needed for sin; He is the King God said would reign; He is the great deliverer from our enemy; and He is the proof of resurrection life that is coming for all those who believe in Him! As 2 Corinthians 1:20 puts it, "every one of God's promises is 'Yes' in him."

If you are wondering today if God is truly faithful, look at Jesus! For in Him, God fulfilled every single one of the promises He made in the Bible. God made good on His Word, through His Son!

On top of that, consider these biblical truths to encourage you about God's faithfulness:

- He is faithful when we are not (2 Tim. 2:13).

- He is faithful in the hard times (1 Pet. 4:19).

- He is faithful to forgive us (1 John 1:9).

- He is faithful to help us through temptation (1 Cor. 10:13).

- He is faithful to guard us from the evil one (2 Thess. 3:3).

Now that we've looked at some Scripture, let's shift our eyes to our day-to-day life. I mean, have you ever just stopped to think of your past life compared to your present and wondered, *How did You get me from back there to right here, Lord?* I know I have. I can recall all the times I had to see my parents fight and the many times I slept afraid something terrible might happen during the night. I remember feeling helpless, and you know what? The Lord guarded me from harm. He brought me through the dark nights.

In another example, I remember sitting under a window on a couch and suddenly, a block-size rock came flying over the top of the sofa, just missing my head by centimeters. (Drugs and alcohol make a parent do crazy things they aren't aware of in the moment—things they wish they could take back—and that was true of my parents in those days.) I remember asking God, *Why? Why must I deal with this?* Yet the faithfulness of God can reach *far*—as far as a story like mine (and yours!). His faithfulness is not just for the people with tidy stories and fun childhoods. It's also strong enough for those of us who faced confusion and trauma. It can reach anyone in any sort of darkness!

Those sleepless nights and confusing moments, weren't the end of the story. Eventually, around the time I was in sixth grade, my father chose to give up his addictions—he wanted a new start with our family. He wanted to leave our home in Mexico and go to the United States, where he could have distance from his past temptations and build a new life. We had given him many chances before, so my mother knew I needed to have a voice in the decision on whether to accept his repentance and receive him back into our family or hold the boundary and keep our distance. If I chose a new life with my family in another country, this would mean leaving all the people I knew—my mom's family, my school, everything. *Stay in this country or go to a new one. Stay here and keep a boundary between you and your dad, or go to the U.S. with your dad and your family together, as one unit, facing a new world together. Hold the boundary or give him another chance.* A hard choice for a sixth grader!

I chose to forgive my dad and take a chance on a new life. It was so scary. Even though I was entering such a beautiful country, the experience felt so intimidating. I came with just some luggage—nothing personal, no family pictures, no toys, no diaries. I came, knowing that I would never see my family members, or grow up with my cousins, never see my house again. But all the while, I knew something in my soul was telling me it was going to be okay. Something was telling me not to fall in fear. That was the faithfulness of God, leading me on.

So we arrived in San Bernardino, California, on an early, foggy Fourth of July in 2001. There was no turning back. My old home had been sold. It was us and God now, in a totally new world. And you know what? My faithful God established me every step of the way. It was hard, but I knew that wherever I would go, my faithful God would be there with me. And somehow, some way, He would make a path for us. And He did! As I've already shared earlier in this devotional, I eventually dedicated my life to God, my dad became a believer, I met my husband, we run a Christian company together, and I eventually founded Fruitful Girl as a way to encourage women everywhere that *God is everything He says He is and more!* We also serve in our church and have three little kiddos running around too.

I know these stories from my childhood are hard to hear, but I share them to help us all remember this: God's faithfulness is not something that only shows up in the sunshine. It meets us in the rain. These stories remind me that God will always show up before and during our desperation—He's never late, but always reveals His faithful hand at the right time!

Whether it is in the story of my mom's struggles, my dad's addiction (and later, his salvation!), or my own memories of darkness, over and over I have seen God's hand of faithfulness and Him always being a provider in time of need. He covered us. As I look back, I see that God was keeping

His promises, even in the moments I couldn't see it clearly. In all the ways Scripture says He is faithful (look back at the list above), He has proven Himself true in my real life!

Our faithful God will establish you and guard you in His faithfulness. He has done it for me, and I can't promise you what the results will look like in your life, but I can encourage you with my own story and say this loud and clear: HE IS FAITHFUL TO YOU. *He is always working, and He is not done yet.*

PRAYER: Lord of lords, I come to You once again to praise You for Your character, especially Your faithfulness toward me. Your faithfulness brought me here, to this day. You know the winding road that led to this day, and all the obstacles and dark nights I've had to overcome, and You gave me strength to keep going every step of the way. You've provided in the hard times. You've forgiven me every time I've run to You in fear or shame. You've seen me through temptation after temptation. You've remained true even when I've felt faithless. Thank You for being such a faithful God! Teach me to be faithful too. I believe You'll establish Your plans for me, no matter what! In Jesus's name, Amen.

REFLECTION QUESTIONS

What typically tempts you to believe God is not faithful? How do you usually respond to that temptation?

Look at the list of ways God is faithful above. How have you seen God prove this to be true in your life?

Why is it so important for you to behold God as faithful in your life before you strive to be faithful toward others?

What does His faithfulness inspire you to do? Can that thing be done for His glory?

UNSWERVINGLY FAITHFUL TO THE LORD

FAITHFULNESS // DAY 2

Let us hold fast the confession of our hope without wavering, for he who promised is faithful.

HEBREWS 10:23 (ESV)

Have you ever felt a deep sense of urgency about something? Maybe it was something serious—like a call from a doctor's office with news of a loved one that you needed to share with the rest of the family immediately. Or maybe it was on the lighter side—something as funny as a long plane ride and *goodness*, did you have to go to the bathroom!

I've learned that urgency tells on people. What we display urgency over is what we typically value most.

In Hebrews 10:23, we are told to hold "without wavering" to our confession. Other translations say "resolutely," "firmly," or "unswervingly." I think we'd all agree that we want to hold on tight to the hope we have in Jesus. And if the fruit of the Spirit is faithfulness, we'd all agree we want that fruit in our lives. In the same way He's held onto us in faithful love, we want to hold onto Him. The question eventually becomes, *How do we know if we're holding in an unwavering way? How can we tell if our grip on our faith is loose or tight? How can we tell if our faith is held fast, or if it's wavering?*

We all want a heart like Peter's when he cries out that he'll never deny Jesus (Matt. 26:35). But the truth is, it's really easy to move away from our faith, becoming the very same Peter who denies Jesus three times! *Why is the wavering so easy?* First, because it's not popular to be a Christian. The world punishes us, whether in overt ways or subtle ones, for living out of alignment with its values. This is pressure we have from outside ourselves to hold our grip loosely on Jesus.

Second, we face many struggles inside ourselves too, one of which is laziness or weakness. In a culture of comfort and constant entertainment, it is not easy to have a discipline toward reading and studying God's Word, which is the very thing we need to remind ourselves of the truth and the hope of our faith!

In order to spot any wavering faith within ourselves, it is really important to pay attention in our actions, reactions, and decisions. Those are all surface-level things going on in our lives, and really, if we trace them down deep, they spring from what's going on in our hearts (Prov. 4:23). These things tell us if we are wavering back and forth between the false hopes of the world and the true hope of our faith in Christ. What does your external life show about what you value? Look at your time—what do you spend it on? Look at your debit card—where does it swipe most? Look at your mental energy—where does it dwell?

Here's another way of saying this: where do you feel that feeling of urgency? Is it when you buy a new gadget and want to post about it all over the Internet? Is it when you get that text message you've been waiting for, and jump at the chance to write back? Is it that last work task you just have to get done, even though you know you should have put up a boundary with your personal time?

If we're Christians, we should hold most tightly to Christ. We should feel most urgent about Him. It's not that the other stuff doesn't matter or isn't important. *But do you still have that feeling of urgency about Him?* The urgency to know God and to let Him be known?

This sense of urgency compels us to seek Christ for who He is and ask Him to clarify anything He wants us to adjust in our lives to live more in alignment with Him, and it keeps our mind fixated on what we can do to further His Kingdom. And you know what else it does? It confirms and certifies us as true believers. If we say our hearts hold a confession of faith, but we never experience an urgency to make good on that confession in the actions of our daily lives, then we need to question if our faith is even real. After all, our urgency to walk out the faith with our works does not save us, but it certainly tells on us! It reveals if our conversion was true.

Just think about it in terms of a story I heard once in a sermon. Down a back road in the country, the son of a farmer was in a field, standing next to a cart. He was struggling to lift a large haystack back onto the cart after it had fallen off. Just then, a rich man from the city came walking down the back road and observed the young man laboring so hard to move the haystack. "That looks exhausting, son! Let me help you—why don't you stop for a few moments?" The young farmer declined: "My father would not allow for that."

"Well, that's ridiculous," said the rich man. "All who labor this hard should get a rest every now and then! Here, have some of this gourmet sandwich and a bottle of my finest drink, too." The young farmer looked longingly at the meal, but shook his head. "My father would not like that, trust me. He wants me to lift this haystack. I don't have even a minute to give." Finally, the rich man got annoyed. "Your father sounds terrible. Point me in his direction—sounds like he needs to be knocked down a peg or two!"

The young farmer said: "Sure, be my guest. You can speak to him face-to-face as soon as I lift this haystack off of him. He's below it, waiting for me to lift it."

Do you see the principle of urgency here? The world will dangle the delicacies of this world in front of our faces, trying to tempt us away from the task at hand. Don't get me wrong—being a Christian doesn't mean we must starve! But we cannot expect the world to understand the urgency of our task, or those who hang in the balance as we seek to know Christ and make Him known. What looks like a crazy amount of labor totally changes when we realize just how urgent the task is, and the souls all around us who are affected by our faith.

It is not wrong to be passionate about many things. But if you and I are more urgent about those things than we are about our Christ, then the Scripture would say we are holding fast *to those things*, not the Lord. If you want a faith that is unswervingly faithful to Jesus, check to see if you're urgent about Him and about the task of making Him known. And if you aren't, good news, my friend—look at the rest of the verse. "He who promised is faithful." If you need help staying consistent in your Bible reading, ask Him. He is faithful! If you need help discerning how to move His kingdom forward, ask Him. He is faithful! If you need His Spirit to search you and change you, and if you need fresh passion and urgency, *He is faithful to help you.* After all, He knew the distractions we would face and how hard it would be to follow Him and stay faithful to our confession. We become faithful because *He* is faithful, He doesn't waver toward us, and He is able to make us like Himself. Isn't that the best news—He is faithful to us in helping us be faithful to Him! With a promise like that, we'll always have what we need to hold fast.

PRAYER: Faithful Jesus, I thank You for the reminder to hold unwaveringly to my faith in You. There are so many things fighting for my attention and loyalty—so many temptations telling me to be more faithful to them instead. Help me hold fast to You above all else! Spark new urgency in my heart to seek Your face and become Your messenger to all those around me. Where I am wavering in my faith or showing more urgency for lesser things, reveal it to me, and fill me with renewed resolve and confidence in Your gospel! In Jesus's name, Amen.

REFLECTION QUESTIONS

What are you most urgent about these days? (Give specific examples.) Why do you think you're so urgent about these things?

Think of seasons in your journey when you were most passionate for Jesus. What did urgency look like for you then?

How can you cultivate fresh urgency for the Lord in this season?

_____

_____

_____

_____

_____

_____

_____

_____

_____

_____

_____

_____

_____

_____

_____

_____

_____

_____

_____

_____

_____

_____

_____

_____

_____

_____

_____

_____

_____

What can you do when you feel your faith begin to waver?

FAITHFUL TO GOD WITH THE LITTLE THINGS

FAITHFULNESS // DAY 3

"One who is faithful in a very little is also faithful in much, and one who is dishonest in a very little is also dishonest in much."

LUKE 16:10 (ESV)

What woman in Scripture captures your attention and awe? Which one do you aspire toward? For many, it's Deborah—a well-known prophetess, a respected judge, a mighty leader for the troops of Israel. For others, it's Lydia, a successful businesswoman who offered her large household to the Philippian church as their base of operations.

There's nothing wrong with holding these women high in our imaginations and valuing their stories—God certainly did great things through them! However, I just wonder . . . would anyone answer that question this way: "The poor widow of Luke 21! The poor widow is who I'd want to be for sure!" Sadly, I doubt it. She's one of those stories we typically forget. And yet Jesus had some high and mighty things to say about her. Do you remember how the story goes?

> While Jesus was in the Temple, he watched the rich people
> dropping their gifts in the collection box. Then a poor widow
> came by and dropped in two small coins. "I tell you the truth,"
> Jesus said, "this poor widow has given more than all the rest of
> them. For they have given a tiny part of their surplus, but she,
> poor as she is, has given everything she has." (Luke 21:1–4 NLT)

This poor widow offers a lesson to us all. She was so faithful with what she had—an amount the world considers little. Yet instead of keeping it to herself, she gave it all to God.

Have you heard about that recent poll revealing that 54 percent of sixteen-year-olds in the U.K. would like to be famous instead of having a real job?[1] Said another way, if these teens believed in God, they'd want Him to put them in charge not of little, but of *much*—much attention, that is.

Or consider this fact: In 1978, being rich came in 8th place among all the goals listed for first-year college students in the U.S. Now being rich ranks number one![2]

As the days go by, it seems there is a higher and higher percentage of people who base their worth on either how many followers they have on social media (fame) or how high the balance is in their bank account (money).

But treating this like a new problem is not the way to handle it. Jesus told stories about money and fame often because people have always struggled to find their value and identity in these things instead of in Him. I think this is because we tend to forget we aren't owners in this world; we are managers of stuff that belong to Someone Else. It's God's world! All the resources of this world are created by Him and come from His hand. So in the end, *He's* the one who should get the fame, not us!

How can you tell if the Spirit is growing the fruit of faithfulness in a Christian's heart? Look for the believers who treat their whole life like it isn't their own. Whether it's their home, their money, their time, their relationships, or their influence, they operate like a steward, not an owner, and they joyfully give it all over to the Lord just like the widow did. They aren't asking, "What more can God give me?" But instead, "What more can I give God?"

And you know what else? They aren't waiting to be faithful until more comes along. They are faithful *right now*. Even if they only have two small coins to rub together, like the widow, they are faithful with them. They steward the little they have for God's glory instead of stalling or rationalizing or tightening their fist.

Here's the truth for us all: if we're tightfisted with the little we have, we'll be tightfisted with more. If we think we can't start being faithful to use what God has given us until more money or more fame comes along, then if it does come, we won't have any muscle memory built up to give it away.

As the Spirit works in us, we will be good stewards of the little we have. I must remind myself of this truth again and again as a Christian businesswoman. I must remember that God can use anything for His glory, no matter how little or how much. Everything is valuable in the eyes of the Lord, and He can be glorified in the smallest of offerings!

My husband and I had to learn this early in our marriage. Though we didn't have much, we chose to give God the little we had back in 2011. Since that wasn't a ton of money, we decided to offer up any talents given to us by Him for His glory. My husband was a graphic designer, and though he could work for any other brand (which isn't a bad thing to do!), He chose to give his gifts to God and use his talent for God's purposes, making Christian apparel that believers could wear out in the world to hopefully share the good news of the gospel more clearly. I helped out and offered up the little I knew about business. Together we helped each other work toward one objective: glorify God and build into His kingdom. We had nothing to our name. We lived in a one-bedroom with a newborn, in a home with our extended family. My husband worked three different jobs, not counting freelancing on the side, all while I was part-time in school and a new mom. My husband did much of the work with website development and design. I tried as best I could to help with production and licensing. We did much of the things ourselves from beginning to end, and we just trusted in God's faithfulness through it all. We gave Him our "loaves and fish" and simply asked God to do something with them—to multiply our offering.

Shortly after this season, God opened many doors for us to get our first home, and He also gave us the strength and know-how we needed to truly run our business well. I don't know what else to say other than God answered our prayers; He used what little we had and He multiplied it! The brand we manage now is called RISEN APPAREL, and it is doing so wonderfully, though we could never take any credit for it.

We didn't have money, so we gave God our talents. All of them. This decision has changed our lives. And the success story isn't that we have a cool business or that we're making money or anything like that. We still depend on God every day! Rather, the success story is we learned how big our God is. He really can multiply the little into much, but *you have to give Him the little*. And it is hard. It feels risky. But it's worth it!

Honor the Lord in the little things you have to offer Him. He doesn't ask you to have a million followers to serve Him, nor does He ask that you make a certain amount before you start giving to His church or His causes in this world. He simply asks for you to make room for His Spirit to open your hand where it was once closed. He asks that you are faithful to offer the "two coins" you have, whatever they are, and believe that He finds those offerings dearly valuable. Whatever it is, don't hold it back—for that would reveal you serve the god of fame or the god of money. *Give it to Him*, and serve your true Lord, *Jesus*, for this sort of faithfulness is a mark of His Spirit. Whatever it is, however hard it is to hand over to Him, know this: He is faithful and He will multiply it.

PRAYER: Oh Lord, thank You for being a God who is so faithful to multiply the little amount Your people give you! I ask that You grant me an honest heart right now—help me see where I'm holding the "little" back from You, and reveal why I'm doing that. I pray that Your Holy Spirit will open my hand in any ways it may be closed. I pray You'll help me entrust my money, time, resources, influence, and everything else— whether it's a lot or a little—to You, and help me be faithful with it and use it to glorify You. You have given me so many gifts; I offer them right back to You to further Your glory. Produce faithfulness in me today, especially with the little things. In Jesus's name, Amen!

REFLECTION QUESTIONS

Have you ever considered the widow in Luke 21 as a hero in the faith? Why or why not? What does she teach you about faithfulness?

What "little" things are you tightfisted with or holding back from giving the Lord? Why do you think you sometimes struggle to believe He'll multiply it?

_____

_____

_____

_____

_____

**What small things are you lacking faithfulness in,
assuming they are too small a deal for God to
care about, or perhaps too "beneath you"?
What "bigger things" are you hoping
He'll give you? Why do you think
you favor those bigger things
over the smaller things?**

_____

_____

_____

_____

_____

_____

_____

_____

_____

_____

_____

_____

_____

_____

_____

_____

_____

**Which parts of your
life do you typically handle
as an owner instead of a steward?
What would change look like for you
as you move toward faithfulness in the
little things?**

_____

_____

_____

_____

FAITHFUL
TO OTHERS

FAITHFULNESS // DAY 4

"Who then is the faithful and wise servant, who his master has set over his household, to give them their food at the proper time?"

MATTHEW 24:45 (ESV)

Have you ever watched the show *Downton Abbey*? (Or maybe another show where there is a large household and everyone has to play a part to make sure the household runs smoothly?) In *Downton Abbey*, there's a head butler named Mr. Carson, and his whole life is dedicated to making sure the Abbey runs as it should. The house doesn't belong to Mr. Carson—it belongs to Lord Grantham, the owner. But no one person can make a whole household flourish, so Mr. Carson along with a cast of other colorful characters all play their important parts to ensure the household hums along in all the ways it should.

As it turns out, *Downton Abbey* isn't the only household that needs a lot of people to do their part! In Bible times, there were large households too, with many colorful characters who stewarded their specific roles to make sure the household flourished. There were cooks and gardeners and cleaners and so forth. So it makes sense that in Matthew 24, Jesus happens to be talking about such a household. His listeners weren't like us nowadays, we who hear "household" and think of the few people in our immediate family. No, His listeners would have known that a household included *a lot* of people, some related to one another by blood, some not, but all committed to the greater task of running an estate well.

Jesus speaks of a master who sets servants over his household. That master is God. And the key mark of the servants who run God's estate? *Faithful.*

But what makes up the household of God, according to the Bible? Chairs and trinkets and big paintings? Are those the kinds of things God wants us to fret over? Nope! If we look at Scripture, we realize the household of God is less about stuff and more about *people* (Eph. 2:19; 1 Pet. 2:5)! When God gives us a part to play in His household, He's primarily giving us a role in the lives of *others*. So faithfulness in God's household means faithfulness in our relationships with them.

Jesus teaches that a faithful servant is the one doing her job well, whether or not the master happens to be physically present. She knows her master is always watching from above. She is taking care of the master's people, and she is not wasting time because she knows that the master can show up at any time, and knows where to find her depending on the hour of the day.

And what would her work look like? If tending to God's household means tending faithfully to the people inside it, how would the Bible tell us to do such a task? Thankfully, it tells us many ways! Just consider the "one anothers" scattered all throughout Scripture. Honor one another, forgive one another, greet one another, pray for one another, serve one another, speak truth to one another, bear one another's burdens, encourage one another, spur one another on, fight for unity with one another, love one another, practice hospitality with one another, be generous with one another—*that's* what faithfulness toward others looks like as servants of Christ!

Let me ask you a question: if our Master came back right now, what would He find us doing in His household? Hanging out in the game room watching Netflix while the other members suffer under some burden outside on the stoop? I don't ask that to place blame, but to give us all a good check on our hearts. How do you want to be found by the Master? If He walked in the room right now, what would He say you are up to in His household? The "one anothers"? Because Scripture is clear—this is what the faithful servant looks like. How do you want to be found?

Here is the good news: the Spirit is committed to bearing the fruit of faithfulness in you, including this kind of servant-faithfulness in the household of God. Here are some questions that might help you cooperate with His work in your heart: Do you serve at church or in your community? Are there needs you might meet in your Bible study group? Are there any gifts you might use to build up others in His household that you are holding back? Is there any form of selfishness God might want to uproot so you might be better equipped to serve others?

I know He's done that in my life! This lesson has been especially hard for me because I was an only child for a long time. I can be selfish. Here's a funny story to prove it: while I was dating my husband, he took me to a theme park and he bought one big chocolate treat for both of us to share. But I didn't know that. He handed it to me, and while he wasn't looking, I ate the whole thing by myself! True story! It didn't even cross my mind to think of someone else. My natural inclination was to *be* served by someone else, not to serve them. And the truth is, we're all wired this way. We need the help of the Spirit to become faithful servants who care about the needs of others in God's household more than our own.

The wonderful truth is this: Yes, there are days we feel like saying, "I hope the Lord doesn't return right now because I'm complaining or slacking, and you know what? I really don't care!" But there is also a powerful God who can change us. His Spirit can turn us into people who say, "I cannot wait to tend to the Master's house and His people today! Lord, come quickly and see how they are developing. See how they are being made ready for Your heavenly dwelling!"

Our promise today is that God's Spirit *will* help us! He *can* change us. He *can* produce faithfulness in us, making us those who are faithful toward others in His family. He *can* develop us into those who are ready for our role in eternity, where we will dwell with God in His household forever, playing whatever part He has for us. Yes, He can!

PRAYER: Heavenly Master, I thank You for inviting me into Your household! I cannot believe I have a part to play in it. If I have not been a faithful servant in Your household in some way, please reveal it to me. Develop me into a faithful and a wise servant who serves You and Your people with all my heart. Help me become ready to be found by You, and give me the eyes to see opportunities to better serve my brothers and sisters in the faith. I pray for the day I'll finally be ready to meet You and hear "well done, faithful servant." In Jesus's name, Amen.

REFLECTION QUESTIONS

If the Master returned right now, what would He find you doing? Do you feel like you're ready to be found?

_____

_____

_____

_____

_____

_____

_____

_____

_____

_____

_____

_____

_____

_____

_____

_____

_____

_____

_____

_____

_____

_____

_____

_____

Are there habits or places that you've been dwelling in where you _wouldn't_ want Him to find you? How might you avoid them in the future?

_____

_____

_____

_____

_____

What are some evidences of God's Spirit developing you in this area? Asked another way, what are some "one anothers" you've been practicing lately—proof that the Spirit is truly changing you, little by little? Are you out of practice in any of the "one anothers"? How might you take a step toward practicing those?

Look up
Hebrews 6:10.
How does this verse
encourage you regarding
faithfulness in the household of God?

FAITHFUL
TO THE END

FAITHFULNESS // DAY 5

"But if you keep on being faithful right to the end, you will be saved."

MATTHEW 24:13 (CEV)

Sometimes I come across passages in the Bible and I wonder why they are there. With this one, sometimes I have thought to myself, *Who in the world doesn't want to be faithful to the end? Who goes into relationship with Jesus with an intentional plan of giving up? No one!*

But then I remember—verses like this exist because we need the reminder! Because as good as our intentions are, and as wonderful as our conversion stories are, continuing in our walk of faith is hard. Many have said that being a Christian is a glorious thing, and it is, but who said being a Christian would be easy? Jesus warns us that we should expect backlash from this world on His account (John 15:18–25).

Though we should expect great joy in walking with our Lord, we should also expect to be pointed at, talked about, blamed for some things, and even persecuted at the hands of those who do not walk with Him. We will be hated for what we believe, for what we stand for, and who we stand with—Jesus Christ. Has this stuff ever happened to you? For many of our brothers and sisters overseas facing death for their faith, this isn't a "will happen" or "might happen" sort of thing, but rather an "*is* happening" thing. We have much to learn from them, for they are living out this very truth. They are remaining faithful until the very end.

Though none of us would wish a terrible fate on any of our brothers or sisters in Christ, the truth is that the fate of the persecuted isn't actually the worst to choose from, biblically speaking! The Bible says it's more dangerous to be lukewarm about God than it is to be a martyr for Him. God has some hard words for the apathetic and indifferent types of

Christians—He says He will spit them out of His mouth (Rev. 3:16)! *Yikes*, am I right? Another way of talking about this is through the analogy of a race. Paul uses this illustration to show us we must finish our Christian race well. He wants for all of us to be able to join Him at the end of our days on this earth saying, "I have fought the good fight, I have finished the race, I have kept the faith" (2 Tim. 4:7). And isn't that what we all want? To step out of this life and into the next being able to exhale and know . . . *I was faithful.*

Paul gives us a beautiful picture of what confidence at the end of our lives might look like. It's not that a Christian should boast in how awesome they were in their earthly life, but rather, they should boast in the Lord—that He brought them all the way to the end, and even when it was hard, they endured. They stayed the course, through the Spirit's power. I hope we all have the confidence and excitement and relief at the end of our journey to feel the very same way.

I hope you don't feel afraid thinking about the end, about Christ's return. If you do feel a bit shaky about it, ask yourself why? What do you need to make right? A believer should be ready to meet the Lord and excited for this fallen world to pass away so that a new, pure one might be established. Paul was confident that he would meet Christ face-to-face, that he would be resurrected just like Jesus, and that a new world awaited him. I am excited about that too! Aren't you? Death doesn't have to make us afraid because we know where we are going. A Christian knows her citizenship is in heaven!

So what will help us get there? What will help us stay faithful in the race? If you're a runner or an athlete of some kind, you know the answer: endurance. Endurance is really important because a long race has ups and downs, various kinds of terrain, and don't forget all sorts of weather! As I've mentioned before, I was a runner years ago, and I have run my share of races. Every single one of them was different. And sometimes, there's no way to tell what's around the bend. In the end, what mattered was not that I knew exactly what was coming, but rather I kept training to build my endurance. If I had endurance, I could finish any race, rain or shine, foggy or clear, mountain or valley.

This applies to our own race of faith. We can't possibly know what's ahead each day, am I right? We can't know if the next season holds rain or shine, rough terrain or smooth roads. Every day, every season, is different. What matters most is for us to build endurance to finish the race, whatever it holds. Endurance is what helps us stay faithful to Christ to the end.

That all makes sense to you, I bet. It makes sense to me too. The hard part is not just agreeing that endurance is the key to staying faithful, but *developing* the endurance to stay faithful! This takes all manner of strain and struggle, of weights and practice and moments of feeling out of breath. Endurance is hard to develop! But we have a great God who is committed to producing this in us. Remember, the fruit of the Spirit is *the Spirit's* thing! He is committed to producing it; our only job is to cooperate with Him. If He is committed to producing a faithfulness in us that lasts to the end, then He is certainly committed to developing the endurance we need to get there. As Colossians 1:11 reminds us, it is according to *His* strength and *His* glorious might that we are able to have great endurance!

Are you wondering how that works? Just look at 2 Thessalonians 3:5—"May the Lord direct your hearts to God's love and Christ's endurance." If you are in need of endurance for your race, the Holy Spirit will direct your eyes to Christ's endurance. He will fix your eyes on Jesus's life, death, and resurrection—all done on your behalf—which will help inspire you to endure too. Said another way: the Spirit of God develops your endurance by reminding you of the Son of God's endurance, and helping you walk accordingly! Don't try to run the race alone. Look to Christ's example, and trust His Spirit to align you to it!

Friend, do not be afraid of the race ahead. Stay faithful. Look to Christ! Remember: trials separate true Christians from false witness. Your salvation will be found genuine during and after your trials and at the end of them as you proclaim honor and glory to the Lord Jesus. Your end is not death, those who keep the faith will be rewarded, and God's Spirit will help you endure in faithfulness to the other side!

PRAYER: Father, thank You for developing faithfulness in me. I pray You will cultivate the endurance I need to make it to the end. Point my eyes to Christ, and reveal anything weighing me down—remove it so I might run more freely toward You. I want to be ready to meet You on the other side of this journey; help me find confidence in that coming day when You return, when You will reward those who were faithful, and when all will be made new. Thank You, Lord, for Your faithfulness that gives me complete trust in Your Word and promises. In Jesus's name, Amen.

REFLECTION QUESTIONS

When you think about the end of your Christian race, what fears do you hold? Why?

_____

_____

_____

_____

_____

_____

_____

_____

_____

_____

_____

_____

_____

_____

_____

_____

_____

_____

_____

_____

What types of things do you sometimes view as annoyances or unanswered prayers, when in truth, they might be things that are developing your endurance? Write down some instances on the lines provided.

_____

_____

_____

_____

Of the verses explored in today's devotional, which one encouraged you most? Why?

REFLECTION AND REST

Use the last two days of this week to rest from reading, and instead, reflect on what you've learned. Use the journaling prompts and space below to process and enjoy what the Lord is doing in your heart.

1. What aspect of God's faithfulness did you find most encouraging this week? Most surprising?

_____

_____

_____

_____

_____

_____

_____

2. In what tangible ways do you see the fruit of faithfulness being developed by God's Spirit in your heart and actions? Take some time to thank God for this fruitful work He's doing in you.

_____

_____

_____

_____

_____

_____

_____

3. In this season of your life, which of these needs the most development in your heart? Circle one.

**Faithfulness to the Lord.   Faithful with the Little Things.
Faithful to Others.   Faithful to the End.**

What are some practical next steps you can take to develop this?

_____

_____

_____

_____

_____

_____

_____

_____

_____

_____

FREESTYLE REFLECTION

Use this space below to pray, write out a meaningful passage of Scripture, or process anything God has placed on your heart this week.

GOD'S GENTLENESS

GENTLENESS // DAY 1

"Take my yoke upon you, and learn from me, for I am gentle and lowly in heart, and you will find rest for your souls. For my yoke is easy, and my burden is light."

MATTHEW 11:29–30 (ESV)

Have you ever read this verse and wondered what a "yoke" is? I don't know about you, but I didn't grow up in an ancient culture that uses a beast of burden to till soil! Nowadays, we have tractors to do this. But back in Jesus's day, the way soil was tilled was to use two oxen who were fastened together by a yoke, a crosspiece, laid on top of both of their shoulders. The yoke would attach to a tilling instrument the oxen would pull through the dirt. It wasn't an easy job. The oxen had a heavy load to pull with that yoke on top of them.

Thankfully we are not oxen carrying a heavy load. With our Christ, though we once carried a big load of sin and extra burdens, He has delivered us from any heavy load in our life. He has exchanged that heavy burden with His light yoke. He is the only One who can offer true rest to our heart and soul.

Are you carrying something heavy by yourself today and want to unload it today and finally find that rest? Christ welcomes you to do so! And what sort of posture does He have toward you when you approach Him with that burden? He tells you: "I am gentle." Of everything God, in the flesh, could say about Himself in this moment, He chooses to say that He is *gentle*. That's how He treats you when you come to Him with a heavy load! *Gently*. And isn't that exactly how you'd want to be treated in such a weary state? How good is our God that, at His core, He is gentle?

Jesus is able to take any weight from us and give us rest, but there is a part we play too. We must first actually come to Him with our burden. And then when He takes our burden from us and gives us His love and instruction in return, we must *follow* that instruction, committing to His will for us as we walk alongside Him. This means we turn over the control of our life to Him, letting Him carry what we once tried to control, and obeying what He says to do. When we do this, we'll find that His instruction for us is good and fruitful and rewarding.

What burden do you struggle to turn over to Him? Where do you assume He'll tell you to do something that, in the end, isn't good for you? Remember, friend, He can be trusted with that burden, and He is a good teacher. More than that, He has the patience and gentleness and instruction we need to grow.

The best teacher in the world, Jesus Christ, is meek and lowly. When we take His yoke upon us, we will find ourselves bearing similar fruit in our own hearts and lives. There will suddenly be no place for harshness or pride in us, but only room for humility. If we truly believe He is Lord, we will follow His humble footsteps, choosing to serve others just as He came to serve us.

Early on in my life as a Christian, gentleness took a while for me to learn. I had plans of my own, and I was a go-getter with lots of goals. I knew what I wanted, and I was going to make it happen! Because of my mentality to "crush my goals at all costs," I was proud and harsh. I wanted nothing that the Lord wanted for me. Well, I suppose I should say I wanted many of His blessings—but not all of them. As I've mentioned before, I wanted everything He had to offer except a marriage or family (knowing me now, many of my current friends would probably find this hard to believe, but it's true!). I rejected one of the most sacred gifts in the world because of my past hurt. I didn't want my children to suffer like me, and I didn't want to suffer like my mother. Even though the Lord wanted these things for me, I did not want them for myself, and so I resisted Him. I didn't bring Him my burdens, trusting He'd be gentle with them. I didn't pray in meekness over what *He* had in store for my future plans. I lacked humility and I let my harshness take over—even boasting about it. I assumed I knew best and carried all my burdens by myself, trying to be successful without Him.

Thank the Lord He is not like us! When we operate like the world does—harshly and proudly—He is not that way in return. He remains gentle. And so, slowly and gently, God gave me the courage I needed to trust Him with my burdens and fears. He helped me see how far He went to save me, dying on the cross for me, which showed me just how trustworthy He must be with not only my present, but my future. Over time, He pushed past my fears, and because He knows me better than anybody or anything, He gave me the true desires of my heart (Ps. 37:4). I finally gave Him my yoke, and I took His. He gave me a marriage and a family—the very things I was afraid of—and through them, He has taught me a deeper love and understanding of who He is. He was gentle with me the whole time, teaching me that walking with Him means we must take *all* His gifts and not just the ones we pick and choose.

Now don't get me wrong. I'm not saying marriage or family, in and of themselves, is the guaranteed reward God gives those who come to Him with their worries. I'm simply saying that I gave Him *my particular* burdens, and in return, He gave me the ability to humbly obey Him where He was leading. I don't know what that might be for you. I don't know what burden you are carrying, and which path God might lead you down. I don't know what His future plans are, or what He's asking you to trust Him with. What I do know is this: He's trustworthy. He's a *gentle* place to run with all your burdens. And whatever load you're carrying, you should surrender it to Him, believing that wherever He leads you is good, and that He's able to give you rest for your soul. Stop fighting against His current—which is something much harder to do than simply obeying and trusting Him!

Friend, surrender it right now. Jesus, who is gentle and lowly in heart, will not punish you or nag you. He will bless you and help you find your way back to His will. He will open up the heavens with the right desires for your heart. He will honor your humility and forgive you as you confess all you've been trying to carry on your own, and He will help you take His light and easy yoke. Take the time you need in this moment, and surrender to His help and His will.

PRAYER: Jesus, thank You for being such a gentle Savior and Lord. I forget so often that this is Your posture toward me when I am weak and weary! Oh Lord, You know the places I am harsh and proud right now. Please change me! I surrender the burden I've been carrying around—You know exactly what it is and for how long I've been trying to bear it all by myself. Right now, I lay it down and give it to You. In return, I pray You'll give me Your light yoke, and rest for my soul. Would You point out the way I should go from here? Help me hear Your instruction and help me follow the path You have for me. Help me believe the plans You have are better than I could have come up with! Above all, I pray You'll give me a gentle and lowly heart, like Yours. In Your name I pray, Amen.

REFLECTION QUESTIONS

What heavy burdens do you carry today? Why do you think you try to carry these on your own? Why do you think you are a better burden-bearer than Jesus?

_____

_____

_____

_____

_____

_____

_____

_____

_____

_____

_____

_____

_____

_____

_____

_____

_____

_____

_____

_____

_____

_____

_____

_____

_____

_____

How does it change things to know that God, at His core, is _gentle_?

_____

_____

_____

In what situations do you tend to be harsh or proud?

In what ways is God giving you opportunities to be gentle, like Him?

WHAT GENTLENESS REALLY LOOKS LIKE

GENTLENESS // DAY 2

Do nothing out of selfish ambition or conceit, but in humility consider others as more important than yourselves. Everyone should look not to his own interests, but rather to the interests of others. Adopt the same attitude as that of Christ Jesus.

PHILIPPIANS 2:3–5

Yesterday we learned that our God in the flesh, Jesus Christ, has a certain attitude toward us. A *gentle* one. And so it stands to reason that if gentleness is found in the heart of our God, we should find it developing in our own heart as His Spirit makes us more like Him. The fruit of gentleness should be bearing itself out in our lives in all sorts of ways! After all, if we're really following Jesus, then as Philippians 2 says, we should "adopt the same attitude" as His. If He has a gentle attitude, then we should as well.

But what does gentleness really look like? If it were to show itself in our lives, how would we spot it? Does it look like being nice? Passive? Condoning?

Thankfully, we aren't left to wonder. Philippians 2 not only tells us to adopt the attitude of Christ; it gives us a clear picture of what Christ's gentle attitude really looks like: *humility*. When it comes to how humility takes shape in our lives and relationships, I love how this paraphrased translation puts it:

> Agree with each other, love each other, be deep-spirited friends.
> Don't push your way to the front; don't sweet-talk your way to
> the top. Put yourself aside, and help others get ahead. Don't be
> obsessed with getting your own advantage. Forget yourselves
> long enough to lend a helping hand. (Phil. 2:2–4 MSG)

That sounds hard to do, right? Everywhere we look, the world tells us to adopt a totally different mindset, one that is set on getting to the top, using your advantages for your own gain, and thinking of yourself first. Some days, it's so hard to remember why we should go the opposite way, why we should let the Spirit bear a different kind of fruit in our life. To help us remember, Philippians 2 holds Jesus's kind and gentle humility out in front of us:

> Think of yourselves the way Christ Jesus thought of himself. He had equal status with God but didn't think so much of himself that he had to cling to the advantages of that status no matter what. Not at all. When the time came, he set aside the privileges of deity and took on the status of a slave, became *human*! Having become human, he stayed human. It was an incredibly humbling process. He didn't claim special privileges. Instead, he lived a selfless, obedient life and then died a selfless, obedient death—and the worst kind of death at that—a crucifixion. (Phil. 2:5–8 MSG)

Ultimately, Philippians 2 helps us remember gentleness is worth it because gentleness looks like Jesus, period. He came to earth as both God and man, and although He had the same level of power as His Father in heaven, He chose not to exploit that and lived in such a way that He had nothing on earth to call His own. From a worldly point of view, He had nothing to His earthly name yet from heaven's view, He was the richest man alive. Jesus was born with nothing, so we could have it all. This is His humble, gentle heart. Going low so we could be elevated. From His ministry of healing and feeding and teaching, all the way to the cross where He saved us, He was selfless, sacrificial, and serving. A King walking among us, dressed in humility. Imagine what the world would be like if all Christians operated this way in their daily lives!

Have you always met the mark in this area? I sure haven't. I'll never forget what our marriage counselor said to my soon-to-be husband and me: "If you think you are humble, and it comes out of your mouth, you're probably not!" She was right. Bragging about your own humility only proves you are actually proud! After saying that, the counselor asked for us to talk about humility not in ourselves, but instead, to talk about it by describing the *other* person's humble qualities. After listing out the ways I see gentleness and humility in my husband, I realized that I considered him the most humble man I have ever met (apart from Jesus, of course). I realized he was selfless, and to this day, that is one of the most attractive things about him to me. That exercise was so great for me. Through it, I learned that humility is something for others to point out and see in you, not something you should point out to others about yourself.

Like Jesus, we should dress ourselves in humility every day. Like Jesus, though we have the same status as those around us—we are worthy, valued, and important to God just like they are—we should not exploit this position of value, but instead use it to elevate someone else.

I think back to my younger years and wish I could have understood this back then. I used to take such pride in my medals in high school. Now, there is nothing wrong with achieving a goal or winning at something you love—that's not my point. The part that was wrong for me is that I wanted all the medals for the wrong reasons. I wanted them so I could get patches to fill up a letterman jacket. Why? Because a letterman jacket filled to the edges with awards and patches meant I'd be admired by my peers—that I'd be *above* them, everyone looking up at me as if I were someone more important than they. If I'm honest, I had selfish ambitions. Any chance I got to bring my medals to a sports day or pep rally, I took it.

Problem is, this strategy never fulfilled me because I always wanted more. No matter how many medals or patches I got, I always had to win *just one more*. And when I did, *just one more*. And then, again, *just one more*. The cycle went on and on, and I didn't realize it at the time, but all that effort was given not to develop as an athlete, but to get people to like me.

This approach to success doesn't end in high school, as you probably already know. We can do this with all sorts of things well into adulthood. Whether it is striving for success in our jobs, our hobbies, or our kids, if we aren't careful to check our hearts, we'll end up in a place where we're doing it all not to *serve*, but to win. To be seen. To be admired or validated. To end up at the top, in front of everyone, so that they might think we're super important.

In the end, although I had the medals that would eventually get me some patches to put on a letterman jacket, I couldn't even afford the jacket itself. God did not allow me to get what I wanted. And now, looking back, I see why. He was protecting me from the path of exalting myself, which would not only harm me, but those around me who I probably would have stepped on to get that jacket. Instead of letting me exalt myself, He humbled me (Luke 14:11). He was showing me the better path of Jesus, my gentle and humble Savior.

Maybe there's some situation in your life where you're facing something similar to what I faced—where you think your heart is going in with good intentions, but really, you're in it for the wrong reasons, and you end up in the wrong place. Friend, I *still* find myself in those places. Here are some questions I ask myself in those situations: *Why do I want to do it? And who do I want to do it for?*

Let me gently ask you this, friend to friend: is your answer "for God and others"? If that's not your honest answer (and many times, if we're real with ourselves, *it isn't*), then don't go another step further until you've worked it out with the Lord. And because we *all* need this reminder, let me put it in front of you clearly: working it out with the Lord shouldn't feel scary. Remember, *He is gentle* toward those who have been trying to go at things alone. He is gentle toward anyone who comes to Him for help when they are caught in something they no longer want to be caught in. If you're realizing you aren't so humble, if you feel caught up in pride or the endless race of getting ahead and climbing the ladder, go to the Humble One. He can help you, and He *wants* to release you from the prison of pride. He can grow the fruit of gentleness and humility in you, *and He will do so gently*.

Although I certainly don't always get it right these days, I can honestly say that in my current life as a growing believer, I have learned to let our humble Savior lead me gently, so that He might enable His gentleness and humility to pour out of my life into others. I have learned that nothing will give us life like He can—not medals or patches or letterman jackets or whatever else. People, pleasures, attention, admiration—none of it can fully satisfy, and when we trust in it for our worth, all of it requires us to become prouder and prouder instead of gentle. I've learned that I have a choice: I can race to the top, or I can walk along a different path, trusting that He "leads the humble in what is right, and teaches the humble his way" (Ps. 25:9 ESV).

I pray for you and for me today, that God would transform our minds and help us think of others before we think of ourselves. As He does this, we will find that we are becoming, a humbler, gentler, and safer place for others. We will find that we're becoming the type of believer who associates with those who can't give us credit or status—the type of believer who lives in harmony with others instead of stepping on top of them. The type of believer who looks like Jesus.

PRAYER: Lord Jesus, thank You for being such a humble and gentle Savior for me. You could have grasped for status and glory, but You lowered yourself so that I might be exalted. You did not go the route of selfish ambition, but instead, chose the path of sacrifice and selflessness. I pray You'll reveal any place I am operating in selfish ambition or conceit, and help me adopt Your attitude instead! By Your Spirit, develop the fruit of gentleness and humility in me, I pray. Open my eyes to any person (or group of people) I am stepping on in order to climb higher, and help me go lower, like You did, in order to serve them and lift them up. In Your name, Amen.

REFLECTION QUESTIONS

With what kind of attitude do you typically begin your day? How does this compare to the attitude of Christ?

In your own words, what does it mean that Jesus is gentle and humble?

"Selfish ambition," for me, looked like filling my letterman jacket with patches that made me look good in front of others. What does selfish ambition look like for you? (Be specific.)

_____

In what ways might
God be developing you
in humility or gentleness?
How can you better cooperate
with the way He is developing this
fruit in your life?

A GENTLE ANSWER

GENTLENESS // DAY 3

A gentle answer turns away anger,
but a harsh word stirs up wrath.

PROVERBS 15:1

Have you ever been in the middle of a conversation, and it didn't go as expected? Meaning, it turned from a *conversation* into a full-blown *argument*? Yeah, I am sure everyone has found themselves spouting off a harsh statement, and typically when we do that, things just go from bad to worse. Feelings get hurt, old wounds open up, and sometimes relationships end up fractured—family members or friendships can even stop talking to each other.

We've all been in some sort of situation like this, and we all know what a hurtful situation it can turn out to be. Trust me, I've not only seen this sort of thing play out in the house I grew up in for many years, but in my own home and in my own marriage in recent days!

How recent, you ask? As recent as writing these very words to you! Lately I've been swamped with work and my writing, and my husband has been a big help. Whether it's taking care of household tasks, helping with certain parts of our business, or tending to the kids, he's been pulling extra weight so that I can finish writing. I am so grateful for his support, but I don't always show it the way I should! For example, on one of my writing days, I was at home working. The kids wanted to go somewhere. My car tends to be the easiest one to take—it requires less gas than his car, and all the car seats are in my car. So, I tell the kids I'm all right with stopping work for a short time and taking them somewhere.

Now, let's pause right here and explore how getting gas works in my mind. Typically, I get gas every two weeks for how much I drive. And, I know it sounds crazy, but I don't really look at the gas gauge all that often. Given our weekly routines, I can just sense when we're coming up on two weeks, and I pull into a gas station to refill. Like clockwork, it always works. Well. *Almost* always works.

Back to the day I was writing and my kids unexpectedly wanted to go somewhere. I stopped working, and I took them. But I didn't account for the extra trip in that week's gas calculation. This new trip, along with a couple other trips in the following days, deviated from our usual two-week schedule. Eventually, our car was running on fumes. And I didn't notice at all until a day or so later, when I picked up the kids from school. After picking them up, I saw the gas light go off, but I needed to rush back home to make it to a meeting. I told my husband I would put gas in the car the next morning.

The next morning comes. My sweet husband took the kids to school so I could sleep a little longer. And guess what? He got a little ways down the road, but had to turn around and come back because there was no way he was going to make it all the way to their school! Once he got back home, he took the kids out of my car and put them in his car, and started the journey toward their school all over again.

Once the kids were settled at school and he returned to our house, while I was working, I could hear his frustration, mixed with some attitude: "Babe, why don't you pay attention to the gas in your car?"

After that, I didn't want to hear him anymore. The weird part is that he was right. I should have paid more attention to the gas gauge! But instead of admitting this, I got defensive. He kept talking, and I tried very hard to hold my anger and my breath. I was listening, but the whole time I was really just trying to hold my feelings back. Did it work? Not really! Eventually, with my own hefty dose of attitude, I blurted out: "Babe, then don't use my car." As you can imagine, where there was once space for an adult conversation, a childish argument now began to emerge.

Looking back, I know that from the beginning of the conversation, both my husband and I should have chosen a gentle answer instead of a harsh word, as Proverbs tells us. On top of that, I should have been prepared for the fact that my trigger was probably going to get pulled (for me, a word with a little bit of attitude behind it makes me feel defensive—it's my trigger). When that trigger is activated, I go into fight-mode more quickly.

What is it that triggers you? What makes you angry? Why? If we know our triggers, we will be able to clearly identify when someone is playing with it, and instead of responding just like the other person, we can respond with a gentle answer instead. In this way, knowing your trigger helps you practice self-control within the situation before it gets out of control and helps you respond with humility instead of snark.

The power of the tongue is strong. As James tells us, words can bring life or death to the heart of another person. And the person who is growing in the fruit of gentleness will use her words to bring life and softness, not death and harshness. Who we are in an argument—that's when the true fruit shows itself! That's when the fruit of gentleness bears itself out not just in theory, but when it's hard—when we naturally want to be defensive or when we feel the impulse to lash out. When the fruit of gentleness is growing in big ways, we'll notice that we use the power of our words not to hurt others (even in moments we feel like they deserve it), but to build others up!

Eventually my husband took the high road and practiced the biblical instruction to use gentle words with me. And you know what? We reconciled. He was sweet and humble, which lowered my defenses. He apologized for his attitude, and I apologized for my rudeness (and I promised to pay more attention to the gas light!). We forgave each other.

The Proverbs are right—a gentle response has a way better shot of ending a fiery argument than harshness does. A humble, quiet, life-giving word is surprisingly powerful. It has the power to turn away anger and make room for love, to persuade the strongest of people and break through the hardest defenses (Prov. 25:15). This is one way the fruit of gentleness works itself out in our lives. In the places the world would flare up in anger at a trigger being pulled, God's gentleness inside of us helps us respond in tenderness. It helps us not say anything harsh, but instead, speak in humility and love. It helps us apologize right away if we need to. It helps us use the kind of power that the world doesn't understand, and enjoy peace on the other side of an argument.

PRAYER: Heavenly Father, thank You for showing me the power and wisdom that comes with a gentle answer. In so many ways, You've won me over with Your gentleness. I don't know why I try to win my own battles any other way. If You win people over with gentleness, why do I try to do this in harshness? Why do I think that will work? I pray You'll develop more gentleness in my responses to others, especially when I feel an argument coming on. Help me see the power You have given me to stop anger from doing damage before it's too late. Help me identify my triggers, so I'll be ready to respond in gentleness when they get pulled. In Jesus's name, Amen.

REFLECTION QUESTIONS

What arguments have you been in lately?

_____

_____

_____

_____

_____

_____

_____

_____

_____

_____

_____

_____

_____

_____

_____

_____

_____

_____

_____

_____

_____

_____

_____

_____

_____

_____

_____

Would you say the fruit of gentleness showed itself in the way you responded? How so, or why not?

_____

_____

_____

How have you seen a gentle answer change things?

_____

_____

_____

_____

_____

_____

_____

_____

_____

_____

_____

_____

_____

_____

_____

_____

_____

_____

_____

_____

_____

_____

_____

_____

_____

What are your triggers? How might you better prepare for them in upcoming conversations?

_____

_____

_____

_____

A GENTLE CORRECTION

GENTLENESS // DAY 4

Brothers and sisters, if someone is overtaken in any wrongdoing,
you who are spiritual, restore such a person with a gentle spirit,
watching out for yourselves so that you also won't be tempted.

GALATIANS 6:1

Have you ever broken something made of glass? If so, you probably know
how hard it is to glue it back together. It's almost impossible because the
glass is so fragile and shattered.

When someone in our life is in the wrong, we often forget how fragile
they feel in the moment we confront them. Or, on the flip side, when
someone confronts *us* for doing wrong, the unexpected conversation can
feel like such a blow, can't it?

Whether the wrongdoer is someone else or ourselves, the "hit" can
feel shattering. Yes, we need to know when we're in the wrong. Of course
we need to be aware and corrected. The right thing to do is to own up to our
mistake and face whatever consequences come our way. But that moment
the issue is raised to us—it always stings.

I love this passage from Galatians, because it seems like the Bible
picks up on this experience. The Bible assumes we (or anyone else) are
in a vulnerable state after being confronted about sin or corrected in a
mistake. And it reveals another way the Spirit bears out the fruit of gentleness in our lives—being gentle in confrontations.

One thing that helps us remain gentle with each other is to remember
that no matter how terrible the other person's particular sin, *we're all
capable of that very particular sin.* Look back at the passage. It says to
"watch out" as we gently correct a brother or sister in the faith, "so that
you also won't be tempted." Why else would the Bible raise up this kind
of warning if it didn't assume you are just as capable of falling into the
same thing the other person fell into? God knows your heart is susceptible

to the same temptations that took down your friend, so be aware and on guard. As the well-known saying goes, the ground is level at the foot of the cross. Whatever your fellow believer is caught up in, you could easily be caught up in as well. And if you were, wouldn't you want someone to gently correct you and restore you to freedom? Of course you would—and so would I! Agree with the Lord, and assume you're no better than your fallen friend, and walk into a corrective conversation as one who wants to help them delicately escape their situation, not join them in it.

So, as we correct our brothers and sisters, let's remember that the pieces of shattered glass all around them call us to be careful. Don't cut yourself trying to pick up the pieces. Just as you would handle shattered shards of glass in a delicate and gentle way, treat your broken brother or sister in the same gentle way. And don't try to clean up the pieces alone! You might miss a piece. This is why seeing ourselves as the body of Christ is so helpful. The church gives us extra help as we handle a friend who has fallen in some way. For the person who fell into sin, standing back up requires them to lean hard into those around them as they figure out their footing. So don't try to be the only one—that's a lot of weight to bear. Share the load with a community of faith who can help this person turn from whatever foolishness they were walking in, and walk in wisdom again. We are the body of Christ, and the best way the body works is by working together. Together we can lift our friends out of the pit with much more strength than if we tried to pull them out alone.

As we've already seen, you and I would want to be treated gently if we were caught in sin and needed help escaping. That's one reason we should handle a corrective conversation gently. But the main reason we should do this is because *God* has gently corrected us and restored us. We serve a God of correction and restoration! Why would we not follow His lead?

Can you remember a time when God corrected you? Restored you? I'm sure you can, because the Bible tells us that "the Lord corrects those he loves" (Prov. 3:12 NLT).

He gently does this. He has for me! And I'm willing to bet you have experienced it. Maybe you are experiencing it right now and can't really see how it will prove fruitful (correction never feels good in the moment!). Maybe a wake-up call has come your way, and the Spirit is revealing to you that you're the person caught in some sort of temptation or sin, and you need to reach out to those who might gently restore you and ask for help. What a miracle! If you are in this place, and you see it for what it is, *praise God*, because eyes to see your own sin is impossible without God opening your eyes and moving in your heart. If this is you, do not be afraid. God is helping you finally see something that has been entangling you, and more than that, He is helping you finally see that He wants to help you escape it and be free! Go and reach out to a leader—someone whose life clearly bears God's fruit, someone you look up to and trust in the faith, someone who you know will give you gentle advice on how to handle this thing that has ensnared you. Don't try to go at this struggle alone! Find accountability (or maybe, lately, it found you) and trust that God's posture toward your heartfelt repentance is gentleness.

Or, maybe you're on the other side of this equation. Maybe you see a friend caught in sin, and God has commissioned you to be the safe place for them to confess their struggles. Maybe God wants you to be the "someone" who a fallen friend looks to and trusts for gentle advice. Let me ask you: When your friend is caught in sin, are you gentle in the ways you respond to this? I'm not saying you should turn a blind eye. I'm saying in your efforts to correct and restore, are you delicate? Careful? Gentle? Compassionate? Because here's the truth: that friend caught in sin, some-where deep inside, *they know it*. They may not have eyes to see it clearly yet, nor the strength to fully repent for it. But if they are living outside of God's design in some area of life, they can sense it deep down. They might suppress it, ignore it, rationalize it, or deny it, but the knowledge of sin is somewhere in there. The way to handle this is not to blow up, lash out, or win an argument. It is to pray that God gives them eyes to see and a heart that breaks for what their conscience has suppressed. It is to give mercy and grace to your brother or sister. As 1 Corinthians 4:21 (ESV) says, "What do you wish? Shall I come to you with a rod, or with love in a spirit of gentleness?"

And let's say your prayer is answered and they *do* realize their sin, and after you have a gentle and corrective conversation with them, they even say they are sorry. How do you handle them after the fact? Do you hold them at arm's length, assuming they'll just do it again? Do you treat them with less honor or dignity compared to those in your life who, in your view, are "getting things right"? Perhaps you have enough compassion for the first go-around, assuming it deserves the gentle approach, but if this issue comes up again? Well, clearly you need to be ready and waiting with a rod in your hand to ensure the message gets across this time. Right?

Wrong. When a brother or sister repents, we should welcome them with open arms and let them get right back to their race of faith. Once we gently restore them—and sometimes the restoration may take some time—we should *continue* treating them gently. Behaving this way is one clear mark of the fruit of gentleness bearing itself out in our hearts and lives—and boy is it hard! Only God can produce this kind of person!

Friend, don't approach anyone with a rod today, but with love and with a spirit of gentleness. The world is filled with strugglers who don't know what to make of the broken pieces in their lives, and they've probably used that rod against one another far too many times. They need someone who humbly and gently reaches out to help (John 13:34–35) with a heart to restore and revive, and they can't do this by themselves. Instead of going the world's way of dealing with those who have wronged you, go the way of God's Spirit, and be part of His miracle of restoration.

PRAYER: Heavenly Father, thank You for being a gentle Father to me when I stumble and fall. Thank You for the ways You have corrected me and restored me in delicate ways. By Your Spirit, help me live this out in my own life and relationships! It can be so easy to go the way of the world, responding to those who fail me in harshness and by lashing out. As I notice any wrongdoing in the life of my friends or family, help me go the way of the Spirit, correcting and restoring them in gentleness and love. In Jesus's name, Amen.

REFLECTION QUESTIONS

How does our surrounding culture deal with being wronged? How is God's way of handling correction different?

What's your first instinct or reaction when you are confronted with your sin? Why?

Can you remember a time God used
someone in your life to correct you
or restore you from a sin that was
entangling you? What was that like?
Who is the first person you call
in a season of struggle? Does
this person have a godly
life? How so?

In this current season
in your life, do you identify
more as a struggler who needs
to reach out to trusted believers
for help, or as the friend of someone
who is currently struggling with sin, and
may need you to correct and restore them?
How might you take a baby step this week
toward what you need to do?

WHEN YOU FEEL LIKE FIGHTING

GENTLENESS // DAY 5

Remind them . . . to slander no one, to avoid fighting, and to be kind, always showing gentleness to all people.

TITUS 3:1–2

I recently had a conversation with my nine-year-old about the power of words. Apparently, there was a video circulating in her circle of friends, and someone on the video used a certain phrase. The thing is, no nobody knows what the phrase truly means, but I could tell it obviously leaned negative in its meaning. So what is a mom to do? I could simply ban the phrase from our house—and now that I think about it, I *did* ban it from our house. But that's not all I did. The power of words can hurt people when they are negative, but they can also help people when they are explanatory, positive, and edifying. So I'd minimize the negative words on the video, *while also dialing up* the positive words between myself and my daughter.

That phrase—everyone thought it sounded funny. Even I had to admit it was catchy, but as I said before, I chose to tell my kids it wasn't a phrase we should ultimately use in our household. Instead of banning this phrase in a harsh way, I tried very hard not to make a big argument about it. I tried hard to gently explain the reason behind the decision. My daughter asked me, "Why can't I say it, Mom?"

I responded: "Do you know what it means?"

She said, "No."

"Sweetheart, why would you say something if you don't know the meaning of it? What happens if you find out after the fact that it was a hurtful thing to say? What if you find out that by repeating it over and over, you've hurt a lot of people?" I told her that words are powerful—they have the power to make you feel good and they also have the power to hurt you.

Eventually I asked her, "How does it make you feel when I tell you how beautiful God made you?"

"Good, Mommy. And loved."

"And how do hurtful words make you feel?" I asked in return.

"Sad, Mommy."

I continued, telling her that words have the power to make people feel certain ways, and so it matters a great deal to know exactly what we are saying.

As a parent, you wonder if meaningful conversations like this sink in, or if they roll right off your kids. Thankfully, most of the time, the teaching moment sinks in—even when you think it doesn't! How do I know? Because later on, my daughter and I turned on our car radio, and the song on the radio said a hurtful word. Immediately my daughter said, "Mommy, let's turn that off because words have power." I realized that she *did* consider my teaching—and more than that, I realized the power of *my own* words with my daughter. The teaching moment worked because it was in a gentle tone!

Whether it's a hurtful phrase on a video or a less-than-supportive conversation you have with a friend about another friend, we all have room to grow when it comes to using gentle words. In Titus 3:2, we see the Bible calling us to "always [show] gentleness to all people." And in the previous days of this week, we've explored what the fruit of gentleness looks like as we show it to all people: serving people in humility instead of stepping on top of them to get ahead, responding in triggering conversations with a gentle answer, and correcting or confronting other believers in a kind and compassionate way. Today, Titus 3:2 helps us discover one other more way the fruit of gentleness bears itself out in our life: avoiding things like slander, fighting, and unkind or hurtful words.

Nowadays, things like slander, fighting, and toxicity are normalized and even expected in friendships and relationships. Sarcasm, tearing each other down, throwing out hurtful and clever phrases, and talking behind one another's backs are the ways of the world. I've even seen social media influencers participate in spouse shaming—laughing at their spouse and trying to make the situation funny, when really, the whole video is built to humiliate a certain weakness or struggle of their spouse. The worst part is that the video encourages other people to laugh along and *participate* in the shaming.

These are all examples of the rotten fruit of the flesh. God calls us to the nourishing fruit of gentleness—something only the Spirit can produce in us. We must remember that ripping someone apart (even if you try to do it in a funny way) does not align with the ways of Jesus, and is unbecoming for a follower of Christ. After all, Christ didn't die so we could tear down His people, but to build them up!

Most of us would agree with this in theory. Who doesn't want to build others up? Who doesn't want to be more gentle and loving? I'd imagine all of us do! So . . . what's the hang-up? Well, gentleness is an easy fruit to cultivate when things are going well. It's when we feel drawn into a *fight* that it gets harder. And these days, there are so many reasons to fight! Arguments around us get so heated in times of political elections, for example. Christians get passionate sometimes, and that's not always bad, but sometimes when you look around (especially online) it's like the call to gentleness is totally thrown out the window! Another example is times of oppression or persecution. When someone seeks to hurt us simply for the fact that we are Christians, our flesh wants to kick back against them with harshness, slander, or even violence. While the Bible gives us plenty of room to build good convictions and even voice them, it does not give room for retaliation. Retaliation is the way of the world, not of the Christian. We are to speak no evil, *even when we see what our enemy is doing*. We are to speak no lies, *even when we're tempted to get back at someone who is doing us wrong*. We are called to gentleness, even when we want to fight. We are called to a higher standard in our conduct toward everyone—the nonbeliever, the believer, the enemy, the influential, or the weak.

If our thoughts and speech shouldn't include things like slander, gossip, or unkind words, what should it include? We are to occupy our thoughts and conversations around the Word of God (Phil. 4:8). When we do, it takes root and it bears good fruit! And can't you tell when someone has done this for years on end? Don't gentleness and love and joy just radiate off of them? I bet you know someone like that in your life. Instead of going the way of a world that fights and slanders and tears down, they went the way of God, and the fruit of gentleness is clearly evident in their life because of it. They don't get pulled in a fight easily. They have gracious words for you in tough times. You can't remember a time they took pleasure in something crude or rude. They are courteous and kind. How beautiful is a person's heart when they have this Spirit-produced courtesy toward others? It's attractive! Those are the sorts of people we like to be around, right? So let's try to be that person for our friends, our kids, and our neighbors. Imagine how different the world would be if we did!

Maybe your mom said the same thing as mine growing up: "If you have nothing good to say, don't say it. Pull back on your instinct to fight and don't say something you'll regret later." And maybe looking back, you can say along with me—*Mama was right.* And so is the Bible. When it comes to our speech (or the videos we watch online of other people's speech!), may we remember our words are powerful and may we replace slander, fighting, and hurtful words with gentleness. Because that is the better way—every time.

PRAYER: Heavenly Father, I worship You and give You all the glory as I consider Your ways, which are so different from the ways of the world! I want to follow Your Word and avoid fighting, slander, and unkind words. It can be so hard when I feel pulled into a fight! As I engage with others, help me do so in gentleness. Instead of breaking bonds with those around me, help me build them stronger and keep them intact. I ask that You help me remember the power of my words and that You'll direct my tongue not only to glorify You, but to build others up, extending courtesy and kindness in the very places the world chooses to fight. In the name of Jesus, Amen.

REFLECTION QUESTIONS

What issue or situation typically draws you into a fight? Why do you think this is the case?

When you fall into gossip or slander, how do you typically feel? (Shame? Regret? Justification? Self-righteousness?) Why?

In which current situations of your life could you replace fighting or gossip with gentleness? Who might benefit from this apart from just yourself?

REFLECTION AND REST

Use the last two days of this week to rest from reading, and instead, reflect on what you've learned. Use the journaling prompts and space below to process and enjoy what the Lord is doing in your heart.

1. What aspect of God's gentleness did you find most encouraging this week? Most surprising?

_____

_____

_____

_____

_____

_____

_____

_____

2. In what tangible ways do you see the fruit of gentleness being developed by God's Spirit in your heart and actions? Take some time to thank God for this fruitful work He's doing in you.

_____

_____

_____

_____

_____

_____

_____

_____

3. In this season of your life, which of these needs the most development in your heart? Circle one.

**What Gentleness Really Looks Like (Humility).   A Gentle Answer.
A Gentle Correction.   Being Gentle When You Feel like Fighting.**

What are some practical next steps you can take to develop this?

_____

_____

_____

_____

_____

_____

_____

_____

_____

FREESTYLE REFLECTION

Use this space below to pray, write out a meaningful passage of Scripture, or process anything God has placed on your heart this week.

THE SELF-CONTROL
OF CHRIST

SELF-CONTROL // DAY 1

Then Jesus told him, "Put your sword back in its place because all who take up
the sword will perish by the sword. Or do you think that I cannot call on my Father,
and he will provide me here and now with more than twelve legions of angels?
How, then, would the Scriptures be fulfilled that say it must happen this way?"

MATTHEW 26:52–54

Do you remember this scene in the life of Christ? Jesus is about to get
arrested and go to the cross, but Peter steps in and interrupts things by
pulling out a sword, trying to defend Jesus from the enemies who have
come to take Him away. Just look at Jesus's response! *Do you think I can't
call My Father right now to get out of this difficult situation, Peter? Do you
think the Father wouldn't give Me an army of angels to defeat all these frail
and feeble enemies in the blink of an eye? Do you think this is all happening
because I can't prevent it—because I'm powerless against it?*

Peter entered a tense situation on pure instinct and impulsiveness. He
thought that the person in the powerful position would be the one holding
the strongest earthly weapon. So he trusted in his sword.

In contrast, Jesus is not impulsive at all. He does not rely on earthly
ways of handling things. And His response to Peter reveals so much,
doesn't it? Jesus isn't in this position because He's powerless against
it. He has more power at His disposal than all the surrounding people
combined! In a moment where you and I would have hearts racing, anxiety
surging, and knee-jerk reactions coming out at every turn, the picture we
see of Jesus is completely different. He tells Peter to put the sword away.
He knows the moment in front of Him is part of His mission, so instead
of letting His previous anguish lead Him to impulsiveness, He responds

with self-control. Instead of exploding or overreacting, He is measured in His response.

Jesus—God in the flesh—practiced self-control. Though He had other options at His fingertips, He chose to respond the right way and in the right measure. Isn't that amazing? Encouraging? Helpful to hear? Self-control isn't just something your Savior asks *you* to practice; it's something *He* practiced as well.

As we read about Jesus's life and ministry, it makes sense that He is self-controlled every step of the way. After all, He is God, and God is self-governing. He has all power—He has everything, really!—and yet He never misuses His power. No matter what the circumstance calls for, He always responds appropriately in every situation. He never overreacts or blows things out of proportion. There are things He *could* do, technically speaking, that He does not do, because He is not one to fly off the handle due to some fleeting, impulsive instinct. Everything He does—every response or reaction or choice He makes—is perfectly appropriate and perfectly measured.

For example, consider 1 Kings 19:11–13, where the prophet Elijah is hiding in a cave. Although there's a strong wind, a massive earthquake, and a hot fire swirling outside of the cave, the Bible says God wasn't flexing His power in those ways. He wasn't in the wind, the earthquake, or the fire, as we'd expected Him to be. Instead, where is God's power? In something as small as a "soft whisper." Don't get me wrong—plenty of other passages in the Bible show God's power displayed in big, flashy spectacles. His power can be seen in those things, depending on the situation. But in Elijah's case, God chose to display His power in something seemingly weak and small. A soft whisper. And doesn't this tell us that God always chooses to handle His power as the situation calls for it? When His people need to learn what it means to fear Him, He sometimes displays His power through thunder or fire or smoke, and the people stand in awe, trembling. (Am I the only one who pictures myself turning into ashes immediately at the point?!) Other times, like this time with Elijah, when His servant needs to develop courage (or perhaps re-learn how to hold Him in awe all over again), God goes a different route. He shows up in a whisper. What does that teach us? That no matter which way He chooses to go, God reveals His power exactly as He should. And He never misuses that power. Whether He blares it from a mountaintop or restrains it down to a whisper, whether He shakes the whole earth or quietly stirs our soul, He is perfectly controlled with His strength.

Given this reality about our God, it makes sense that self-control is a fruit of His Spirit! As we grow in our sanctification, He wants to produce the same sort of thing in us. And boy do we need it! Just take a look around at what humans do with just a little bit of power given to them. Over and over again, fallen humanity has proven to misuse its power instead of being self-controlled with it. Imagine how dangerous the world would be if we were the higher power in this universe instead of God!

Thankfully, God knows exactly how much power and pressure His children need to slowly learn self-control. He knows the situations to put in our lives so that we might become more like Him in this way. Moment by moment, He is training us to walk in all the aspects of His character— love, joy, peace, patience, kindness, goodness, faithfulness, gentleness, self-control—because "against such things there is no law" (Gal. 5:23 ESV).

Where does self-control help us most? In the moments we "can't" or "don't want to" do all sorts of things He is telling us to do. In the moments our knee-jerk reaction would be to, metaphorically, draw a sword like Peter did. For example, sometimes it is hard to love or care for someone who is difficult. Yet, God calls us to love our enemies. Self-control helps us do this! When the fruit of self-control is growing in our lives, we will start to see that we're truly able to rein in our natural response to return evil for evil, and even in the heat of a hard moment, we can choose to *bless* the difficult person! And let me tell you, friend, the world doesn't have power like that! Isn't it amazing the Lord has given us control over our reactions?

If you're anything like me, you know self-control isn't possible unless God is part of the equation. He has to be working in us for self-control to work itself out in our lives, but you know what? We have to be open to working at it too. The process of growing in self-control requires our participation. We have to fight for it every day. So choose self-control today. In the moments we are most likely to overreact or follow our flesh, let's ask God to convict us—whisper to us, even—and help us respond differently. Differently like Jesus!

PRAYER: Oh heavenly Father, thank You for being perfectly in control—not only in control of the world, but totally in control of Your own responses! I confess to You right now that I am not always in control when I react to the situations in my life. I can rely on earthly instinct. I can be impulsive. I can blow things out of proportion. I can go the way of knee-jerk reactions instead of measured, godly responses. You know exactly which situations I have lacked self-control—I pray You'll make me different. Different like Jesus! Help me respond appropriately in all circumstances, and give me power to restrain myself when I feel the desire to be rash. In Jesus's name, Amen.

REFLECTION QUESTIONS

In which area of life is it hardest for you to exercise self-control? Why?

What would healthy self-control look like in this area of your life? Be specific.

_____

**How does it help to know that Jesus
practiced self-control in His earthly
ministry? How does His example
encourage you?**

_____
_____
_____
_____
_____
_____
_____
_____
_____
_____
_____
_____
_____
_____
_____
_____
_____
_____
_____
_____
_____
_____

**How has God
shown His power to
you in very different ways,
depending on the situation?**

_____
_____
_____

DISCERNMENT

SELF-CONTROL // DAY 2

And it is my prayer that your love may abound more and more, with knowledge and all discernment, so that you may approve what is excellent, and so be pure and blameless for the day of Christ, filled with the fruit of righteousness that comes through Jesus Christ, to the glory and praise of God.

PHILIPPIANS 1:9–11 (ESV)

For any fruit-bearing plant, there are always little pests that come in and prevent the fruit from growing as it should. When it comes to the fruit of self-control in our lives, what do you think most prevents it from developing? A lot of people might say "lack of willpower" or maybe "a habit of indulgence," and those answers are true to a certain degree. But you know what "pest" I think people typically forget? A lack of discernment.

What I mean is this: self-control requires you to restrain a bad, inappropriate, or unhealthy reaction in favor of a good, appropriate, healthy reaction. A person with self-control has a certain mastery over their behavior, to the point that they can choose the *right* response over the *reflexive* response.

But think about it: all of that requires a person to know the difference between a right and a wrong response, yes? Self-control can move a person toward appropriate and measured actions (or reactions), but what defines *appropriate*? What defines *healthy*? What defines *good*? What makes something *right* versus *reflexive*? Only a person with discernment can know the difference between these things!

Perfect control over our actions and reactions is natural for God, but it's not natural for us. Sin has entered the picture, and it has distorted our minds and our hearts. We need the help of biblical discernment and wisdom to help us know right from wrong, so that when we practice self-control, we steer our hearts and our actions in the right direction.

Paul's prayer to the church of Philippi helps us learn more about this. After Paul prays for love to abound between believers, he then moves from love to "knowledge." Paul wants them to learn more of the Scripture. Why? Because knowledge of Scripture leads us to discernment. Scripture tells us what's good and what's bad, right and wrong, appropriate and inappropriate, healthy and unhealthy. As we read the Bible with the Spirit of God helping us understand it, we grow in discernment!

This passage helped convict me about why it is so important to read Scripture, not just randomly but daily, so that I might develop discernment for myself. After all, at some point in our Christian journey, we will realize we can't live on one sermon a week. We will realize we need to consume the nourishment of God—His Word—regularly so that we might be spiritually filled up. He wants us to read and understand the Scripture, not just to check off some box, but so that we might be nourished, filled, full of wisdom, and pleasing to Him!

I had to learn to do this when I realized I wanted to share my faith and my lessons-learned with others, but I didn't know how. After all, we can only teach what we know. How could I share my faith when I didn't know much about it? How could I point people to the God who speaks into *their* lives when I wasn't paying attention to the primary way He was speaking into *my* own life—through His Word?! I hope this does not shame you, but rather encourages you. Don't wait any longer to dive into God's Word, friend; start today. I've been in the season where God gave me the push I needed to get to work, read Scripture, and join a Bible study at church. Perhaps He's doing the same with you right now!

If you're wondering which way to go in a certain situation right now, look to Scripture to help you learn the basics of wisdom, because God will use the sixty-six books of the Bible in every season, and you'll find that your spiritual eyes will notice things you didn't see before as you explore. It's amazing what can happen when we learn to be attentive to the wisdom that is available to us! As we make Scripture our guide, we'll grow in our ability to differentiate right from wrong, which is vital for our spiritual growth as believers.

I love how Hebrew 5:14 explains it: "But solid food is for the mature—for those whose senses have been trained to distinguish between good and evil." In another translation, instead of "senses," it says, "powers of discernment." The "solid food" here is Scripture, which means that our power to discern and therefore be self-controlled all comes from knowing the Bible! As newborns in the faith, we start with the "milk" of the gospel, but the Lord expects us to move on to solid food—to His whole counsel throughout the whole Bible.

As we've seen, when we consume more and more of the Bible, we are able to distinguish God's truth from the lies of the world. That means we can then turn around and practice self-control as we choose the way of the truth over and over again, no matter what our flesh or our circumstances or our culture or our friends tell us. This is how we gain greater self-control over any obstacle we face.

Have you ever had a strong season in the Word? I bet when you look back on those seasons, you remember not just *reading* Scripture more often, but *speaking* it more often. And that makes sense, because when we consume it more and more, it naturally pours out in our conversations. I love those seasons. When I think about it, the most meaningful conversations with my husband or my friends are the ones when Bible verses, more than anything else, are flying back and forth among us all. And you know what? I tend to have more self-control in seasons like that! What a great picture of the discernment God is developing.

If you struggle with self-control, don't be discouraged, friend. God is committed to growing it in you as He develops your discernment. Try one small step this week—govern your time toward God's Word, and watch how it helps you not only *distinguish* the wise path, but gives you the ability to *choose* that path with self-control. Even when your fleshly reflexes try to steer you the wrong way, God is sure to grow you into a person who *knows* the right way and *takes* it.

PRAYER: Oh Lord, I want the fruit of self-control to be fully cultivated in my life! I admit to You right now that I struggle with self-control—and You know exactly what area in my life is hardest. Sometimes I fall because I don't always know the right path. I pray You'll give me the strength and resolve I need to stay consistent in Your Word, so that I might grow in my ability to identify the wise, healthy, and appropriate path to take. With surroundings as loud as my culture, it is hard to distinguish between good and evil sometimes, but I pray You'll make it clear to me as I grow in my knowledge of the Scriptures. Listen to my cry and give me the discerning mind You promised. Help me govern my time and my desires, so that I act in self-controlled ways that please You! In Jesus's name, Amen.

REFLECTION QUESTIONS

**Have you ever connected
self-control to discernment?
Why is this connection
so important?**

**In what ways are you
helping yourself grow in
discernment? In what ways
are you hindering yourself?**

What changes are you willing to put in place so that you might grow more in discernment and self-control?

_____

_____

_____

_____

_____

_____

_____

_____

_____

_____

_____

_____

_____

_____

_____

_____

_____

_____

_____

_____

_____

_____

_____

_____

_____

_____

_____

_____

_____

_____

_____

What other believer in your life might be able to join you in this change?

_____

_____

_____

SELF-CONTROL IN OUR SPEECH

SELF-CONTROL // DAY 3

Keep your tongue from evil and your lips from deceitful speech..

PSALM 34:13

As we explore self-control in general this week, I wonder what specific areas of your life are hard for you to restrain. For many of us, if we're honest, we'd rather control other people instead of ourselves, am I right?! For example, you might be thinking, *Restrain? I wish I could restrain my rambunctious kids!* Or, *I wish I could restrain the constant negativity of my boss!* Or, *I wish I could control the way my clueless neighbor leaves their trash bins outside for weeks at a time!*

But the fruit of the Spirit doesn't end with "others-control," does it? It ends with "*self*-control." So let's turn our attention inward today. In what specific area is it hard for you to restrain *yourself*? There are common answers that people will give to this question—how we respond in traffic, for example, or how we eat, or how we treat others when we lose at something we're super-competitive about. And all of those are legitimate answers. It can be hard to restrain ourselves in those moments! But today let's focus on one area of life many people bypass, or forget about: *our speech.*

David gives us great advice on this in Psalm 34:13—to keep our mouths from evil and our lips from speaking lies. Self-control is implied in this verse—do you see it? He doesn't say, "Ask someone else to make sure you don't use your words the wrong way." He says *keep* your own tongue from being used the wrong way. *Keep* yourself from doing something you shouldn't do with your speech! The Bible would not call us to keep ourselves from something bad if we weren't actually *able* to restrain ourselves—but we are. The Bible *assumes* self-control is possible. Especially with our speech. *We are fully capable of "keeping" ourselves in check!*

I think we'd all agree we want to exercise more self-control with our mouths. We all want to pull back on our bad verbal habits. But many times, we don't take the time to consider where our bad habits *start*. Where do you get your verbal habits from? Well, there are two answers to this.

First, our words start in our hearts. Consider Jesus's words in Luke 6:45: "A good person produces good out of the good stored up in his heart. An evil person produces evil out of the evil stored up in his heart, *for his mouth speaks from the overflow of the heart*" (emphasis added). Our words flow from our hearts. So, if the words coming out of our mouths end up being something we consider problematic, that means there's something going on *inside* of us—something on the heart-level—that's problematic. Our words start with our hearts. So the natural question here is this: What is in your heart? Is there anything in there that is producing speech that is not self-controlled? If you dig deep, is there anger? Unresolved conflict? Bitterness? All these things will end up producing all sorts of unrestrained, ungodly comments to come flying out of our mouths!

On top of our bad verbal habits coming from the things going on *inside* us, they also come from the things *surrounding* us. When I think of our family's life, I realize that so much of our speech comes from the cultures all around us. We naturally start copying the TV-talk. Or my kids easily pick up the way the cool kids speak at school. Or we hear something catchy on the radio (or our favorite music-streaming app). However it comes to us, it is easy to adopt the kind of language that surrounds us.

Who do you look up to? What fictional characters on TV do you spend a lot of "time" with? Do you spend more time hearing from them compared to the time you spend hearing from real-life Christian friends? How do you think that's impacting your view of what's "normal" in your speech? The same goes for me!

Or, if you're not a big TV person, what kind of music are you listening to? How is that impacting your life and your verbal habits? How does that square with the amount of time you spend listening to music that worships the Lord?

Or if you're not into TV or music, here's a big one: How many hours a day do you spend listening to the speech of random people on social media? What is their speech like? How is that shaping the way you use your tongue? I'm not trying to condemn you, friend. I'm just trying to draw our attention to the way our bad habits start so that we might build better habits and make it easier for ourselves to keep our tongues from evil.

Consider the voices you are listening to most often and ask yourself if they are truly voices of blessing. James 3:10 reminds us of something so important: "Blessing and cursing come out of the same mouth. My brothers and sisters, these things should not be this way." The Bible assumes that a person cannot bless and curse at the same time. Or consider a similar, modern saying you might've heard about people who use their words in evil ways: "Do you kiss your mama with that mouth?" The point is clear: we shouldn't be hypocritical in the way we use our words, nor should we listen to people who are. We shouldn't laugh at crude language on social media as we make our way to Bible study, but then switch to "Christian speak" when we walk in the door to the church.

Let's say you struggle sometimes with your speech (and we all do)—perhaps this looks like cursing, or gossip, or inappropriate jokes. When you get "caught" in the act, how do you usually feel? If the answer is "not great," that's a good thing! That means the Spirit is working in you. I give my kids this advice all the time: if you are talking to your cool friends and bad language comes rolling out of your mouth (and theirs), and a teacher hears it, the people in the circle who know they were wrong will say, "I'm sorry." I tell my kids: if you are that person who says sorry, this is evidence of God working in you. It means you care about what God cares about, and you have a higher chance to change than those who feel no remorse! As bad as we feel when we use our tongue for evil, the good news is that we actually feel godly sorrow over it! I've been in this place before, and each time I stumble, I pray and ask God for a controlled tongue and His strength through the Holy Spirit.

If we call ourselves believers, let's commit to using our words the way God would have us use them. Instead of speaking with a dirty mouth, let's trust God's way of handling our tongue when He says, "No foul language should come from your mouth, but only what is good for building up someone in need, so that it gives grace to those who hear. . . . Let your speech always be gracious, seasoned with salt, so that you may know how you answer each person" (Eph. 4:29; Col. 4:6). Let's not just hope for better habits, but fight for them by *keeping* our mouths from evil by exercising self-control. God empowers us to do this through His Spirit. He enables us to do this, and He *believes* we can do this—so let's believe too!

Let the word of Christ dwell richly among you, in
all wisdom teaching and admonishing one another
through psalms, hymns, and spiritual songs, singing
to God with gratitude in your hearts. (Col. 3:16)

PRAYER: Jesus, our Savior and Advocate, You always use Your words for good! You do not curse me and bless me in the same breath. You only bless me. You use Your words to create good things, to defend me, to intercede for me, to encourage me, to correct me, to train me, to help me, to comfort me. Develop self-control in me so that I might use my words the same way! Help me govern my mouth to avoid evil and instead, pursue good. Help me know when to be silent and when to speak up. Above all, help me remember that keeping my tongue in check is truly possible in the strength You provide! In Your precious name, Amen.

REFLECTION QUESTIONS

In what ways do you struggle with self-control when it comes to your words? What internal issues within your heart are overflowing into your external speech?

What surrounding influences in your life are affecting the way you speak (think about what you watch, listen to, or read)?

_____

_____

_____

_____

_____

Our society often says we can't help what we say. How does Psalm 34:13 respond to this assumption? How does this truth encourage you today?

_____

_____

_____

_____

_____

_____

_____

_____

_____

_____

_____

_____

_____

_____

_____

_____

_____

_____

What small step can you take today to keep your mouth from evil and encourage others instead?

_____

_____

_____

_____

SELF-CONTROL IN EATING

SELF-CONTROL // DAY 4

It is not good to eat too much honey, nor is it honorable
to search out matters that are too deep.
Like a city whose walls are broken through is
a person who lacks self-control.

PROVERBS 25:27–28 (NIV)

Have you ever had a really difficult season when it comes to controlling your eating? I certainly have. I can remember the middle school years where this was tough for me, particularly one summer break before high school started. New to the United States, I survived two years of middle school. Though I had done a decent job learning a different culture and a new language, I no longer had any structure in my life—which is something middle schoolers need!

This new season just ahead of me—*high school*—seemed so strange and difficult. After literally starting life in a new country during middle school, I now had to start a life all over again in high school, which may as well have been a new country! I did not know how to handle the massive change coming for me. I heard high school was going to be even harder than middle school, and I had to apply what I had learned in my language classes and start practicing my English speech because I was a quiet one. I wasn't quiet because I wanted to be (if you know me, you know I am happy to open up and chat!). Rather, I was quiet because I didn't want to feel embarrassed if I said something wrong with my accent.

With the anxiety of my high school future just ahead of me, it was a stressful summer break. To confront my fear, I started summer school to try and get ahead. Well, it didn't go as I imagined. I didn't realize summer school was for the kids who didn't do so well during the prior year—the kids who, many times, had behavioral issues. I was bullied, repeatedly. I would cry and cry until one day I decided to stay home instead. Home wasn't perfect, but it was better than the bullies.

I didn't leave my room. In the isolation, I ate. I'd eat in my room, snack in my room, and I'd even try to soothe my negative emotions with food in my room too, especially during the middle of the night after a nightmare. I'd wake up in terror, only to eat more, hoping to be filled with comfort.

My mom noticed I was having a hard time. I told her it was school and the new changes. I found a short-lived comfort in eating, but over time, I didn't feel good and even struggled with a dark season of depression.

On a Sunday at church in Sunday school, someone shared that we could bring our feelings to the Lord in prayer. This was when I started praying about my fears—instead of going to food for comfort, I slowly began going to the Lord as a better source of safety and help.

When I consider Proverbs 25:27–28 (ESV), I realize exactly what was happening to me in that season of life. One, I was trying to handle matters too deep for *just* me to figure out. I needed the Lord! Only God can search the depths of a heart and truly comfort the types of issues I was trying to smother with "too much honey." And two, I was operating with no self-control. "A man without self-control is like a city broken into and left without walls." I had no walls, meaning boundaries, which meant I had no protection against any attack. My relationship to food needed boundaries and structure, but I was in a totally structureless phase of my journey.

Over time, as I brought my needs and worries to the Lord, I grew in self-control. I built up those boundaries! Anytime I went to my room, I made sure I didn't take any food but instead, my prayer notebook. Instead of my typical routine of getting snacks and sitting by myself, I started keeping busy, which led me to find healthy activities like track and field. I had never run in my life—I knew *nothing* about running. I tried the long jump because I was too short for the high-jump, and during group drills, I was asked to try out for sprints. That's how I was introduced to running over hurdles. Finding track and field helped me learn even more healthy disciplines, as my team and I managed our schedules and balanced the time it took to complete not just practice times, but school work too. Track and field helped me find a healthy physical outlet for my negative feelings (now I had an alternative; I could hit the pavement instead of the cupboard), but ultimately, it drew me even closer to the Lord as I prayed during my runs and read more of my Bible during my commutes.

Eventually I got out of the dark place, and I credit God for that—for His amazing ability not only to offer comfort to me but also to develop self-control in me! I still look back and stand amazed at the ways He grew me in that season. Just months before I had no boundaries, but there I stood, changed. I still remember when I stopped drinking soda because Coach said it was not good for the bones and for running. I fueled my body with good things, and I stopped eating my feelings away. I started to face my fears, which is exactly what I needed not only to face the start of high school, but also to get all the way through it. These good habits were the grace from God that I needed to say no to all the temptations high school brought my way. All glory to the Lord for saving me from a dark time and preparing me to avoid many other temptations!

I share all of this to encourage you. I don't know what your relationship is to food. Maybe you, too, know what it's like to use food as a comforting friend. Maybe you, too, have had to learn the hard way that "it is not good to eat too much honey" as a means to sort out the deep issues brewing in your heart. Or maybe you're on the flip side. Maybe you're lost in fear of gaining weight and you're resorting to eating far less than you should in order to stay thin, lacking the willpower it takes to consume the standard calories your body needs in a given day. I can tell you as a friend on the other side of that: if you are trying to find a place of rest or comfort or confidence, dear friend, *of course you are*. We all are. But you won't find those things in piles of food. (Nor will you find them in eating virtually *no* food.) Self-control with food isn't ultimately about finding satisfaction in the right diet . . . it's about finding satisfaction in God. Only in Christ can you find everything you need.

When you feel that pull toward the pantry (or the pull away from it when you know you shouldn't be starving yourself), remember that *He* longs to fill you up. Go to Him to be filled, and I promise, He will sustain you and comfort you in much deeper ways than a few bites, snacks, or plates—or lack thereof—can. Because really, we all know that whether we've dodged all our calories in order to be fulfilled with earthly praise or stuffed ourselves full of so many calories that we can't breathe in our jeans anymore, we feel emptier all the same on the other side. I'm not saying, "Don't eat." Nor am I saying, "Just go on a diet." So please don't hear those things. Rather, hear this: lift up prayers to your Father before you lift your fork. Feast on His Word, your Daily Bread, before you feast on the food. You will feel fuller with Him, I promise.

You and I need comfort, and we also need structure. The sweet honey of God's Word, but also boundaries. And God has both for us. When we go to Him, we will learn, little by little, how to put those boundaries up and what the fruit of self-control can really look like with food.

> Every athlete exercises self-control in all things.
> They do it to receive a perishable wreath, but
> we an imperishable. (1 Cor. 9:25 ESV)

PRAYER: Father, thank You for making food a good gift for me to enjoy. I confess right now for all the ways I haven't treated it that way. Sometimes I treat it as more than a gift—but rather, a god that I run to when life gets hard. Other times I treat it as less than a gift—as a hindrance that gets in the way of my image goals. Please correct my view of food in the moments I feel pulled to treat it wrongly. I need Your help to develop self-control as I walk forward in this area. Wherever I lack boundaries, help me build them, and replace any bad habits with godly ones. Help me run to You above anything else for comfort, rest, confidence, and security. In Jesus's name, Amen.

REFLECTION QUESTIONS

When you think back to a season in your life when you reached out for food too often (or too little), what do you think you were actually reaching out for?

In your own words, explain how a person without self-control is like a city with broken-down walls.

How have you seen small evidences
of God growing the fruit of self-
control in you when it comes
to your relationship
with food?

_____

_____

_____

_____

_____

_____

_____

_____

_____

_____

_____

_____

_____

_____

_____

_____

_____

_____

_____

_____

_____

_____

_____

_____

How might you
better cooperate with God
in the future as he develops self-
control in this area? Are there any
boundaries you need to set?

SELF-CONTROL IN OUR RELATIONSHIPS

SELF-CONTROL // DAY 5

Women must likewise be worthy of respect, not malicious gossips, but self-controlled, [thoroughly] trustworthy in all things.

1 TIMOTHY 3:11 (AMP)

But as for you, exercise self-control in everything, endure hardship, do the work of an evangelist, fulfill your ministry.

2 TIMOTHY 4:5

If you could rank all the things that are most important in your life, what things would make the top 5? The top 3? The top 2? The Bible says that relationships with others are the second most important thing in life, next to our relationship with God. God has made it clear to first love Him with everything we've got, and then secondly to love our neighbor as ourselves, even considering their interests as more important than our own (Luke 10:27; Phil. 2:4).

That all seems simple enough to understand, but boy, do we have a hard time living this out! It seems no matter how hard humanity tries, we just can't love God or others in a totally pure way without selfishness getting in the way, or pride driving a wedge, or disagreements rising up left and right. In so many cases in families and churches, separation and divisions have become more normal than unity! I suppose this shouldn't surprise us when we look back to the beginning.

In Genesis 1–3, we read about the first relationship known to man: the one between Adam and God. And when Adam and Eve fell, there was a new and painful separation that divided them and God. God had to separate Himself from His beloved children, because now they were clothed in sin instead of righteousness, and God only dwells in righteousness. He cannot dwell in sin. So where unity and harmony and intimacy used to be, now there was this massive gulf between the two parties.

Fast-forward to Jesus. In God's Son, Christ, He offers humanity a bridge back to Himself. Back to relationship, back to intimacy, back to unity! Christ paid for the sin that separated us from God and brought us near once more, if we'd only believe in His sacrifice and resurrection. For believers, we are finally united back with God by the blood of Jesus!

Wonderful. Now that we're fully reconciled to God through Jesus, you'd think Christians would be natural reconcilers with those around them, right? If their God went through all that trouble to build a bridge, you'd think they, too, would be bridge-builders every where they went. And you'd be right about one thing—they *should* be. But there's a big gap between "*should* be doing" and "*are* doing." Sometimes God's people need help getting from one to the other. And in His great patience, God is teaching us how to close that gap. He is showing us, day by day, what it actually means that all His children, no matter how different they may be in terms of background, ethnicity, status, or otherwise, are all united as one in Him. He is revealing to us, slowly but surely, the places that still have walls built up—walls that need tearing down.

It is so much easier to remain in a bubble with our favorite group of Christians or even within the walls of our home. We'd rather be left alone. We'd rather not have to deal with anything or anybody else on the other side of the walls we've built. I know because I've experienced this many times! God will call me to reach out to those who live in some other bubble—a bubble different than mine—and I've talked myself out so many times. I was like, "Lord, I know You're calling me to help pull this wall down, but I don't like drama! What if it causes some tension? What if it's hard? What if I'm misunderstood?" But who am I to excuse myself from the command to help others or create unity where there is division?

After a while, I realized the truth: I needed more unity in my life. I wanted community—even the kind that requires me to fight for it—but what was holding me back was fear of rejection. After all, in my growing-up years, I had been rejected so often for my background, my ethnicity, how I looked or dressed . . . I didn't want to try any longer. But eventually I read about Jesus being rejected during His earthly ministry. The Bible revealed to me that Jesus was God in the flesh walking the earth, and He was denied to the point of death! And He did all of that for the very purpose of uniting us to His Father! He chose rejection so we could have unity and reconciliation! Why should I expect any better treatment than that? Why should I be surprised when making peace with others takes work? When we realize rejection is part of the deal in this life, and was part of the deal in Jesus's life, it makes working toward unity so much easier. Not everyone is going to understand us, and that's okay. Not everyone is going to be exactly where we are on things, and that's okay, too.

When I think of how Jesus handled His relationships—especially the relationships that were hard—I realize He had so much self-control. Where He could have demanded His own way or blown up in an argument or even given the cold shoulder, He didn't. And He did this as an example for us. I love how 1 Peter 2:21–23 puts it: "Christ also suffered for you, leaving you an example, that you should follow in his steps. He did not commit sin, and no deceit was found in his mouth; when he was insulted, he did not insult in return; when he suffered, he did not threaten, but entrusted himself to the one who judges justly."

Imagine if we all had this sort of self-control in our relationships! The amazing truth is this: we can. Because the Spirit of Christ lives in us, we, too, can follow in His steps in making peace with others, refusing to insult them when they insult us, refusing to threaten or lash out when they misunderstand us or even turn against us. What self-control this takes! Yet it is possible through the Spirit, who develops this ability in our relationships.

While every Christian is called to self-control in relationships, when we consider 1 Timothy 3:11 and 2 Timothy 4:5, we realized that self-control is especially required in the life of a Christian *leader*. In 1 Timothy 3:11, we see that if a female believer is looked up to in her church, the Bible says she should be someone worthy of that respect. And how do we know if she's worthy of respect? If she is "self-controlled, trustworthy in all things" (AMP). This doesn't mean she never has the wrong desire or impulse, but rather she should be able to govern her actions and restrain those unhealthy impulses by not indulging them, and instead, responding to them by doing the right thing.

In 2 Timothy 4:5, we're taught that Christian leaders should "exercise self-control" not just in a few challenging areas of life, but "in everything." Everything! And what evidence reveals that a Christian leader is actually displaying self-control in everything? They endure hardship; they do the work of an evangelist; they fulfill what God has called them to do, no matter what kind of temptations pull them away from the call. This is convicting for us all, as self-control in our relationships clearly extends to non-Christians. Sometimes when we look around at our lost culture, our impulse is either to run and hide from it or fight with it on every little detail we disagree on. But self-control toward unbelievers looks like doing the work of an evangelist! A self-controlled leader will not give in to the temptation to run or to fight; they'll rein in those knee-jerk reactions, and instead, share the gospel!

Isn't it great news that the Spirit can produce this kind of fruit in us? Isn't it relieving to know we aren't alone in it? When we feel the pull to give in to the impulses of our flesh, *He will help us* govern our response and return evil with good. That's what the Spirit of God is there for! To cultivate this ability in our hearts. Praise be to God!

What are your relationships like right now? Are you exercising self-control in them? Are you fighting for unity in the power of the Spirit when it would be easier to just follow your impulses to stay in separate camps, walls up? Are you showing an example of what this kind of work looks like in your camp, proving yourself worthy of respect among the family of faith? And outside the family of faith, are you doing the work of an evangelist? All these things take a great deal of patience and discipline, which basically means self-control, because we are not wired to do them naturally.

Let's conclude today with James 1:19–20 (ESV): "Let every person be quick to hear, slow to speak, slow to anger; for the anger of man does not produce the righteousness of God." What wonderful verses to guide us in self-control in every single relationship we have. Quick to hear, slow to speak, and slow to anger. What if we could pull back on our inclination to be heard, and instead put our efforts toward hearing? All that energy that boils inside when we feel like we're losing the upper hand, or our rights—what if we channeled that energy to opening our ears and closing our mouths? *That's* self-control, and it can save many relationships before they take a turn toward being wrecked. Whether it's with our kids, our spouses, our friends, our unbelieving relationships, or some other "camp" we don't like, imagine how our relationships would change if we got out of the way and let the Spirit bear the fruit of self-control—and every other fruit—to its fullest!

PRAYER: Lord Jesus, thank You for coming to lay down Your life to bring me back to unity with the Father. You saw when I was separated from God, You didn't run away in fear, nor did You insult me or fight with me. You did the work of peacemaking and helped bridge me back to the Father, even when it cost You Your life, Your reputation, and so much rejection. Thank You for coming near and tearing down the dividing wall! Help me be this kind of unity-builder in my relationships. Through Your Spirit, develop in me the self-control it takes to pursue unity among Your people when I'd rather run away or put my gloves up. And give me the inner discipline required to share the gospel with my unbelieving friends. Help me do the work of an evangelist, especially when I feel the pull to avoid gospel conversations. I am part of Your body, Your hands and feet in this world! Help me, Lord, to prove myself true to the task of godly relationships, and give me the strength to respond the right way, even when I feel my impulses tempting me down an "easier" route. In Your name, Amen.

REFLECTION QUESTIONS

In what way do you most struggle with self-control in your relationships?

_____

_____

_____

_____

_____

_____

_____

_____

_____

_____

Why is unity such an important thing to fight for among Christian communities? How does pursuing this relate to self-control?

_____

_____

_____

_____

Who looks up to you in this season of life, or watches your life? (A church group? Your kids? Your nieces or nephews? Your neighbors? Fellow students? Other moms? etc.) In what ways could you better model self-control in front of them?

Who are the unbelievers in your life? What would self-control look like in those relationships for you?

REFLECTION AND REST

Use the last two days of this week to rest from reading, and instead, reflect on what you've learned. Use the journaling prompts and space below to process and enjoy what the Lord is doing in your heart.

1. What aspect of God's self-control did you find most encouraging this week? Most surprising?

_____

_____

_____

_____

_____

_____

_____

_____

2. In what tangible ways do you see the fruit of self-control being developed by God's Spirit in your heart and actions? Take some time to thank God for this fruitful work He's doing in you.

_____

_____

_____

_____

_____

_____

_____

_____

3. In this season of your life, which of these needs the most development in your heart? Circle one.

Self-Control that Is Guided by Biblical Discernment.
Self-Control in Speech.   Self-Control in Eating.
Self-Control in Relationships.

What are some practical next steps you can take to develop this?

_____

_____

_____

_____

_____

_____

_____

_____

_____

_____

FREESTYLE REFLECTION

Use this space below to pray, write out a meaningful passage of Scripture, or process anything God has placed on your heart this week.

NOTES

Week 7: Day 3

1. Alison Kershaw, "Fame the career choice for half of 16-year-olds," *Independent*, February 17, 2010, https://www.independent.co.uk/news/education/education-news/fame-career-choice-half-16-year-olds-1902338.html.

2. Luke Landes, "Millennials Want to Be Rich More Than Anything," *Consumerism Commentary*, July 23, 2019, https://www.consumerismcommentary.com/millennials-want-to-be-rich-more-than-anything/.

ACKNOWLEDGMENTS

Thank you to my heavenly Father God, for your Son Jesus and for my life and salvation. You have guided me since I was a little girl. I would have never done anything without Your blessing and help. Thank You for the privilege to be Your daughter and for giving me so many promises during the writing process. Thank You, Lord.

To my husband Gerald M. Ramos: thank you for always being my number one supporter in everything I do. You are an amazing son, brother, father, worker, and a true spiritual leader in our family. Also, thank you for letting me be real and making room for our differences. Thanks for the nine plus years of wisdom that you have ahead of me, and for always pointing me back to Jesus. You are my always and forever.

To my editor Ashley Gorman: I appreciate the time you took to encourage me to write this book. Thank you for the common bond we share, and girl, thank you for sharing the writing gift God gave you to better help me say exactly what I wanted to say. Loved working with you and I hope we get to do this again.

To my children Gianna, Gerald, and Gilanny: I hope one day you read this book and see what God has done, and I pray that you keep the faith and run the good race with endurance. Love you kiddos, so much and always!

To my mother, Veronica Mendivil: thank you for giving me the one piece of advice that has seen me through hard times, "Obedience." That is the best inheritance you could have given me. Te amo!

To my father, Francisco Grijalva:. I bless you, dad! God has redeemed us. Te amo!

To my "Tata," Patricio Grijalva: I miss you. Thank you for everything you did for us without expecting anything in return. I still wait for my phone to ring. Rest in peace, and my hope is to see you again in heaven with my Nana. Love you both.

To my college coach, Ken Blumenthal: thank you for being the godly father figure in my life when I needed it the most. God knew. Thank you for teaching me God's Word and protecting me from boys, but saving me the best one you knew. In large part due to you, I now call him my husband.